THE COOKING OF
VENICE
AND THE NORTH-EAST

BONECHI

HOW TO READ THE CARDS

DIFFICULTY	FLAVOUR	NUTRITIONAL CONTENT
● Easy	● Mild	● Low
●● Medium	●● Medium	●● Medium
●●● Difficult	●●● Strong	●●● High

Preparation and cooking times are shown in hours (h) and minutes (e. g. 30′ is 30 minutes).

NOTES AND SUGGESTIONS TO READERS:

IN THE TEXT OVEN TEMPERATURES ARE GIVEN IN CENTIGRADE. THE FOLLOWING CONVERSION CHART MAY BE USEFUL:

150 °C/ 300 °F/ GAS MARK 2
160 °C/ 325 °F/ GAS MARK 3
175 °C/ 350 °F/ GAS MARK 4
190 °C/ 375 °F/ GAS MARK 5
200 °C/ 400 °F/ GAS MARK 6
220 °C/ 425 °F/ GAS MARK 7
230 °C/ 450 °F/ GAS MARK 8

Project: Casa Editrice Bonechi
Series editor: Alberto Andreini
Coordination: Paolo Piazzesi
Graphic design: Andrea Agnorelli
Make-up: Bernardo Dionisio
Cover: Maria Rosanna Malagrinò
Editing: Rina Bucci

Translation: Aelmuire Helen Cleary

Chef: Lisa Mugnai
Dietician: Dr. John Luke Hili

The photographs of the food are the property of the Casa Editrice Bonechi Archives and were taken by Andrea Fantauzzo

Photos on pages 8,28, 32, 44, 104, 110, 133, 134 and 160, property of the Casa Editrice Bonechi Archives were taken by Di Giovine Photo Grafica
The photo on page 50, property of the Casa Editrice Bonechi Archives, was taken by Luciano Casadei
The photo on page 68 was taken by Di Giovine Photo Grafica
The photo on page 80 was taken by Andrea Innocenti
The photo on page 174, property of the Casa Editrice Bonechi Archives, was taken by Gianni Dagli Orti
The titlepage photo, property of the Casa Editrice Bonechi Archives, was taken by Dante Pini
The photo on page 188 is taken from "Le bianche case alla riva" – Genoa

For the photographs with no identified source, the Publisher would appreciate any information so as to integrate reprinted editions.

© by CASA EDITRICE BONECHI, Firenze - Italia
E-mail: bonechi@bonechi.it   Internet: www.bonechi.it

Printed in Italy by Centro Stampa Editoriale Bonechi, Sesto FIiorentino (Firenze)

ISBN 88-476-0753-1

***

THE COOKING OF VENICE AND THE NORTH-EAST

Venice and the Triveneto (the area of north-eastern Italy comprising the three distict regions of Veneto, Trentino-Alto Adige and Friuli-Venzia Giulia) is a land of contrasts: prodigious and thrifty, carefree and Byzantine, rustic and aristocratic, a land of sea and of mountains, jealous of its tradition yet constantly open to renewal. This book is not only a manual of gastronomy, featuring all the specialities of the region and guiding us through the delights of the table, it also accompanies us on our journey through the marvels of art and the beauties of nature. The itinerary is splendidly varied: from the treasures of Venice to the peaks of the Dolomites, from the silent reaches of the lagoon to the rushing waters of the Adige and the Tagliamento, from the splendour of the Palladian villas to the rustic austerity of the *masi* or farmsteads, from the foaming breakers on the Trieste shore to the ripples lapping the reeds at the mouth of the Po.

In the fine city of St. Mark, which seasonally rediscovers its age-old youth through contact with the millions of tourists which throng to pay her homage from every part of the world, the art of cookery flourished amidst the *calli* and the canals, between courtly residences and gossip-filled *campielli*, evolving from a unique blend of aristocratic refinement and folk wisdom. The predominant flavour is that of the sea, coloured by the black of cuttlefish ink, the silvery slither of anchovies and pilchards, the gold of crispy sea fries and the pearly reflexes of the exquisite shellfish. But it also comprises the diaphanous transparencies of the lagoon, the supple vitality of the eels which swim upstream and the velvety softness of the

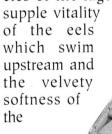

plumage of the water fowl which nest there. The pastries and biscuits, such as the famous *baicoli*, epitomise the carefree joy of Carnival.

At the same time, there is a process of continual renewal. Even recently, the superb classic dishes have been augmented by strokes of genius such as the tasteful and sophisticated *carpaccio*, inspired by the imaginative flair of Cipriani which rapidly became popular throughout the world, and the refined delicacy of *tiramisu*.

Similarly, the cuisine of the Veneto hinterland evokes the flavours of misty fields, vines stretching over sundrenched slopes and shimmering waters. The flavours of Trentino are redolent of rock and musk, of juniper and mushrooms, of the roar of the trout-filled mountain streams, of woods and game, of pastures and milk. Finally, on the tables of Friuli we can taste the sea breezes and the mountain air and savour an atmos-

phere of sincere and simple strength, the same features we find in the *grappa*.

Most of our recipes, especially the more complicated, are accompanied by a series of photos to make them easier to follow. As usual the list of ingredients does not include salt or pepper; their use in Italian cooking is taken for granted, just as that of water for boiling pasta or other ingredients. So, although it seems unnecessary to list them, the recipes do indicate at what point they should be added (preferably in moderation). Salt is only listed in the ingredients for sweetmeats and biscuits, where it is only occasionally used.

Before starting, we recommend that you run through the list of ingredients (which also features preparation and cooking times, indications of the degree of difficulty, the strength of flavour and the nutritional value) and then read carefully the various stages of the recipe itself. After this, all that's left to say is *Buon Appetito!*

LOCAL SPECIALITIES

*S*ince the recipes in this book are grouped by category, it seemed a
good idea at this point to give an indication of their geographical origins, identifying the principal dishes of each area. This will help us to
recognise the culinary traditions of Venice and the various different regions of the Triveneto and enable us, if we wish,
to plan "typical" menus.

Having welcomed us with an appetising array
of cicheti, *antipasti and snacks inspired by the
marine tradition, the enticement of Venice pro-
ceeds with the delights of pickled pilchards,
pasta and beans, rice with mussels or rice and
eels (*risi e bisati *not to be confused with* risi e
bisi *– rice and peas), followed by the famous
Venetian-style liver and rounded off with sweetmeats such as* baicoli *and* zaleti. *A closer ac-
quaintance with the city will then enable us to
savour the flavours and fragrances which*
emerge from its ancient tradition of trade with the Orient, such as those
we can detect in the rice in cavroman *(with mutton), the Greek-style
pilchards and the Eastern-style red mullet. The heady fragrance of the
spices which were brought to the warehouses by ships bearing the ban-
ner of the Lion of St. Mark also pervades the* pevarada, *closely related to
the Veronese* pearà, *a spicy sauce served as an accompaniment to roast
and boiled meats.*

Beyond the Venice lagoon, the fishponds of Chioggia, *famous for
its round* radicchio *or red chicory, are a major feature in the
cuisine of the Triveneto: fish holds sway in the* broéto *fish
soup, in the pilchards and cuttlefish* alla ciosota *– Chiog-
gia-style – and in the famous eels* in tecia *(with tomato
sauce), and game in the* màsaro alla Vallesana.

In the hinterland - dominated by the gilded hues of the
polenta *which reaches its gastronomic apex in the
pastizada and is the ideal accompaniment for game,
as in the famous* polenta e osei *- every town boasts
a wealth of surprises. Padua, famous for its fat hens,
vies with Venice to claim the* risotto alla sbirraglia.
Vicenza and its region regales us with bigoli *with
duck, the superlative Vicenza-style salt cod and the*
bussolà. *Verona, homeland of* gnocchi *triumphs
with the* pandoro, *while Treviso, famous for its long-
leafed* radicchio, *which is exquisite grilled and also fea-*

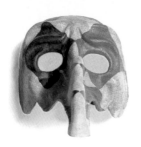

tures widely in risottos and fillings, offers the delights of sopa coada *and* tripe. *From Belluno, on the slopes of the mountains, come delicacies such as the filled pasta* casunziei *and the specialities of Cortina d'Ampezzo.*

Adding a further touch of aristocratic refinement to the food of Veneto are the great wines of the Alpine foothills, such as Bardolino rosso *and* Custoza bianco, *of Valpolicella, Soave and Gambellara, the land of the incomparable* Recioto, *and of Breganze, where we can savour the famous* Torresani *and the noble* Torcolato. *Or again, the nectars of Montello, of the hills of Asolo and Conegliano, where the sparkling* Prosecco *is born, the Colli Berici, realm of the* Tocai rosso, *and the Colli Euganei, famous for* Bagnoli bianco, *to round off with the wines of the Piave, Lison-Pramaggiore and Verduzzo.*

Friuli welcomes us with simple authenticity and dishes which resemble it, such as iota, mocnik, *and the exquisite* sguazeto ala bechéra, *Trieste-style* sole *and, to round off,* struccoli, gubana *and* potizza. *The Friuli fare is enhanced by the inimitable wines of the plain (*Pinot bianco *and* Pinot grigio, Tocai *and* Friuli Verduzzo, Franconia, Refosco dal peduncolo rosso *and* Schioppettino) *and of the hills (*Collio, Merlot, Picolit *and* Pinot nero).

Trentino-Alto Adige, the land of the exquisite speck, *prime ingredient of an excellent bean soup, offers us a filling variety of* canederli *or dumplings, or alternatively proposes the potato-based* Ciaroncié of Moena, *the sophisticated Tyrolese-style stuffed breast of veal and the rustic* tonco de Pontesel, *trout from its streams cooked in different ways, to be rounded off with the familiar* pan dolce *or a superb* zelten. *Here the fine wines feature the distinctive flavours of* Teroldego *and* Müller Thurgau, Traminer *and* Riesling italico *and* renano, Marzemino, Sylvaner *and* Terlano.

DIETICIAN'S ADVICE

The attempt to comprise the cooking of Venice and the north-east within a single regional gastronomic category is a fairly daring operation, as tends to be the case when we try to make schematic distinctions. While from certain aspects it can be generically defined as "northern", the choice of ingredients which range from the Adriatic coast to the Alps undoubtedly make it extremely varied from a dietary point of view.

It is certainly a "northern" cuisine in terms of the wide-spread use of fats of animal origin, rich in saturated fatty acids. This is a distinctive feature of the Alpine culinary tradition, in particular of that of Trento and the South Tyrol. Nevertheless the Mediterranean imprint persists, underlined by the ubiquitous extra-virgin olive oil, a presence which extends beyond the strictly coastal areas, and by the excellent raw vegetables to be found everywhere (with the famous *radicchio* or red chicory of Chioggia and Tre-

viso). The Mediterranean aspect is also revealed by a calorific content predominantly based on complex carbohydrates, although with a strong northern tinge in that these nutrients tend to be less wheat-based, originating rather from corn and potatoes. These features, which we have defined as almost completely Mediterranean, disappear in the cuisine of the South Tyrol, dominated by animal fats and by proteins of beef and pork origin.

INDEX OF RECIPES

ANTIPASTI, "CICHETI" AND SAUCES

1

ACCIUGHE MARINATE

Marinated anchovies

1 kg/2¼ lb fresh
anchovies
1 kg/2¼ lb red onions
Red wine vinegar
Olive oil

Servings: 4-6	
Preparation time: 20' + 5-6h	
Difficulty: ●	
Flavour: ●●●	
Kcal (per serving): 416	
Proteins (per serving): 32	
Fats (per serving): 26	
Nutritional content: ●●●	

1 Wash and clean the anchovies, removing the heads and bones, then split them open down the middle. Peel the onions, and slice them finely. In a bowl arrange alternating layers of anchovies and onions.

2 Season lightly with salt and pepper, then pour over enough vinegar to cover the contents of the bowl. Leave to marinate in a cool place for at least 5-6 hours, or even overnight. The anchovies, which will turn a lovely pinkish colour, should be served drained of their marinade and garnished with a trickle of good quality olive oil.

"BOVOLETTI"

Snails

Wash the snails thoroughly under cold running water to remove all traces of dirt, then set them in a saucepan full of cold, lightly salted water and turn on the heat very low. As the water heats the molluscs will emerge from their shells. When the water comes to the boil, and a layer of white foam forms on the surface, drain the snails (keeping the shells to one side) and garnish with the finely-chopped parsley and garlic and lashings of oil.

To serve, replace the snails in their shells, and arrange on a serving-dish.

If you have gathered the snails yourself, remember that before cooking they should be kept for a couple of days under an upside-down recipient which allows the air to circulate, for example a wicker basket, with a little moistened bread and a few lettuce leaves. After two or three days they are ready to cook.

28-32 snails
3 cloves garlic
Parsley
Olive oil

Servings:	4
Preparation time:	20'
Cooking time:	30'
Difficulty:	●●
Flavour:	●●
Kcal (per serving):	182
Proteins (per serving):	8
Fats (per serving):	16
Nutritional content:	●●●

"CANOCE"

Squills

2 dozen squills (or mantis-shrimps)	
2 lemons	
Parsley	
Olive oil	
Servings: 4	
Preparation time: 10'	
Cooking time: 5'	
Difficulty: ●	
Flavour: ●●	
Kcal (per serving): 172	
Proteins (per serving): 5	
Fats (per serving): 15	
Nutritional content: ●●●	

Wash the squills under cold running water, then scald for 5 minutes in salted water to which you have added the juice of half a lemon. Drain and serve seasoned with pepper and lemon juice, olive oil and finely-chopped parsley.

The best time to buy squills is during the winter months, especially in November and December when they are full of eggs and the meat is firmer.

"GARUSOLI" ALL'AGLIO

Murices with garlic

28-32 murices	
1 clove garlic	
1 bay leaf	
Parsley	
Whole black peppercorns	
Olive oil	
Servings: 4	
Preparation time: 10'	
Cooking time: 15'	
Difficulty: ●	
Flavour: ●●	
Kcal (per serving): 161	
Proteins (per serving): 3	
Fats (per serving): 15	
Nutritional content: ●●●	

Rinse the murices repeatedly under cold running water, then boil them for about 15 minutes in salted water to which you have added a bay leaf and a few whole black peppercorns. Drain and remove from the shells with the help of a slender pointed instrument. Season with the finely-chopped garlic and parsley and olive oil. Replace in the shells and serve cold, garnished to taste.

"PEOCI" RIPIENI

Stuffed mussels

800 g/1³/4 lb mussels	
1 clove garlic	
Parsley, Breadcrumbs	
Olive oil	
Servings: 4	
Preparation time: 10'	
Cooking time: 15'	
Difficulty: ●●	
Flavour: ●●●	
Kcal (per serving): 189	
Proteins (per serving): 8	
Fats (per serving):16	
Nutritional content: ●●●	

Brush and wash the mussels thoroughly. Place them in a saucepan with a trickle of oil and let them open over a rapid heat. Throw away the empty half-shells, and sieve the cooking juices. Chop the garlic and parsley finely, then spoon the mixture over each mussel, sprinkle with breadcrumbs and season with salt and pepper. Pour two tablespoons of oil into a casserole, arrange the mussels in it, then moisten with 3-4 tablespoons of the sieved cooking juices and a trickle of oil. Cover the dish and cook for ten minutes.

These three recipes are all included in the category of "cicheti", antipasti and snacks inspired by the marine tradition (based on "peoci", "caparossoli" and "bevarasse", "garusoli", "capelonghe", "capesante" and "canoce", that is mussels, clams, murices, razor-shell clams, scallops - the French coquilles St. Jacques - and squills). In Venice it is the custom to savour these along with an "ombreta", that is a glass of wine, while waiting to move on to the main dishes.

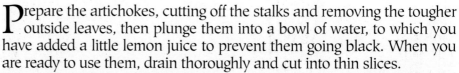

350 g/12 oz calves' brain
4 artichokes
1 egg
1 lemon
Breadcrumbs
Parsley
1 tomato (to garnish)
Oil for frying

Servings: 4	
Preparation time: 20'	
Cooking time: 10'	
Difficulty: ●●	
Flavour: ●●	
Kcal (per serving): 454	
Proteins (per serving): 15	
Fats (per serving): 35	
Nutritional content: ●●●	

CERVELLO FRITTO CON I CARCIOFI

Fried brain with artichokes

Prepare the artichokes, cutting off the stalks and removing the tougher outside leaves, then plunge them into a bowl of water, to which you have added a little lemon juice to prevent them going black. When you are ready to use them, drain thoroughly and cut into thin slices.
Trim and wash the brain and chop it into evenly-sized pieces. Beat the egg, add a pinch of salt, dip in the chunks of meat and then roll them in the breadcrumbs. Fry in hot oil in a frying-pan for 4-5 minutes then drain and lay to dry on kitchen paper. At the same time fry the artichokes in another frying-pan. Add the artichokes to the fried brain, season with salt and sprinkle with finely-chopped parsley. Serve the fry garnished with cubes of fresh tomato.

Fegato "in saór"

Pickled liver

1 Place the liver in a casserole, preferably earthenware, with the chopped carrot, celery, one onion and a bay leaf. Cover with cold water and bring to the boil over a gentle heat. Simmer for about an hour, then leave the liver to cool in its stock.

2 Peel the remaining onions, slice thinly and sauté gently in a casserole in 2-3 tablespoons of oil.

3 Tip in half a litre of vinegar, a little at a time. Add the raisins and pine kernels, allow the flavours to blend for a few minutes, then turn off the heat and leave to rest. Slice the liver and arrange on a serving-dish, seasoned moderately with salt and pepper, and alternating with spoonfuls of onion. Trickle with oil and sprinkle with raisons and pine kernels, garnishing to taste.

400 g/14 oz calves' liver (one piece)
1 kg/2¼ lb onions
Half a carrot
Half a celery stalk
1 bay leaf
50 g/2 oz raisins
50 g/2 oz pine kernels
Vinegar
Olive oil

Servings: 4	
Preparation time: 1h	
Cooking time: 1h 30'	
Difficulty: ●●	
Flavour: ●●●	
Kcal (per serving): 307	
Proteins (per serving): 18	
Fats (per serving): 19	
Nutritional content: ●●●	

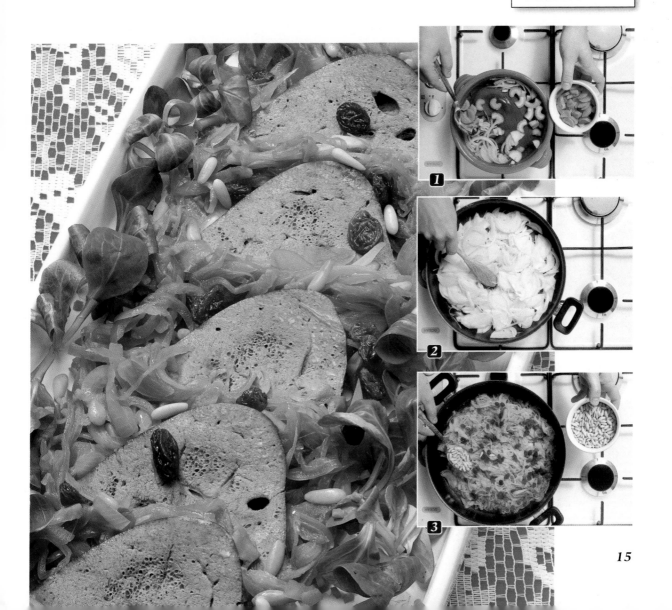

MELANZANE "IN SAÓR"

Pickled aubergines

800 g/1³/₄ lb aubergines
3 onions
30 g/1 oz raisins
30 g/1 oz pine kernels
Red wine
Red wine vinegar
Oil for frying
Olive oil
Servings: 4
Preparation time: 15′ + 24h
Cooking time: 30′
Difficulty: ●●
Flavour: ●●●
Kcal (per serving): 518
Proteins (per serving): 7
Fats (per serving): 39
Nutritional content: ●●●

1 Wash and dry the aubergines and cut them into slices about 1 cm/¹/₂ in thick. Fry them, then lay to dry on kitchen paper and sprinkle with salt.

2 Slice the onions finely, then sauté lightly in a frying-pan in 2-3 tablespoons of olive oil. Pour over a glass of wine and one of vinegar, add the raisins and the pine kernels, and season with salt and pepper. Leave the flavours to blend for 2-3 minutes, then turn off the heat.

3 Arrange alternate layers of aubergines and the onion mixture in a serving-dish, until all the ingredients are used up. Keep in a cool place, and serve the following day.

PÂTÉ RIALTO

Rialto pâté

1 Melt 30 g/1 oz of butter in a small saucepan, then blend it with the flour. When it begins to turn pale brown, add a glass of milk a little at a time, stirring gently with a wooden spoon. After cooking 6-7 minutes, season with salt and pepper and switch off the heat. The béchamel is ready for use.

2 Whiz the liver in the food processor (instead of fresh liver you can also use leftovers of Venetian-style liver – see p. 78 – with the onions removed). Clean and grate the truffle and sauté briefly in a small saucepan in the remaining butter. Gently fold the puréed liver into the béchamel, adding the truffle and butter.

400 g/14 oz calves' liver
1 black truffle
40 g/1^1/$_2$ oz flour
Milk
70 g/2^1/$_2$ oz butter

Servings:	4
Preparation time:	20'
Cooking time:	12'
Difficulty:	●●
Flavour:	●●●
Kcal (per serving):	332
Proteins (per serving):	23
Fats (per serving):	21
Nutritional content:	●●●

600 g/1¹/4 lb pilchards
2-3 spring onions
2 bay leaves
Flour
White wine vinegar
Whole black peppercorns
Oil for frying
Olive oil
Servings: 4
Preparation time: 20′ + 4-5h
Cooking time: 30′
Difficulty: ●●
Flavour: ●●●
Kcal (per serving): 503
Proteins (per serving): 20
Fats (per serving): 41
Nutritional content: ●●●

SARDE "IN SAÓR"

Pilchards "in saór"

1 Peel the onions and slice them finely. Sauté lightly in 2-3 tablespoons of olive oil, a finger of vinegar, a few grains of pepper and two bay leaves. Allow the flavours to blend over a gentle heat for about 10 minutes, without allowing the onions to brown, then switch off and leave to rest.

2 Wash and clean the pilchards, removing heads and bones, then split them open. Coat in flour and fry in boiling oil; drain and lay to dry on kitchen paper, sprinkling lightly with salt.

3 Arrange alternate layers of pilchards and onions in a serving-dish, then leave aside for at least 4-5 hours before use. Serve at room temperature. If stored in a cool place, the pilchards are also excellent even several days later.

SEPPIOLINE DORATE

Fried cuttlefish

600 g/1¹/4 lb cuttlefish
Flour
Salad leaves (to garnish)
Fried polenta (to accompany)
Oil for frying

Servings: 4
Preparation time: 30'
Cooking time: 5'
Difficulty: ●●
Flavour: ●●
Kcal (per serving): 628
Proteins (per serving): 27
Fats (per serving): 38
Nutritional content: ●●●

Clean the cuttlefish, removing the bones, eyes and ink-sacs. Wash them and leave to dry thoroughly on absorbent kitchen paper. Dust lightly with flour and then fry in plenty of boiling (180 °C) oil for about five minutes until golden. Drain and leave to dry on kitchen paper, salt to taste and serve garnished with tender salad leaves and accompanied with fried polenta.

For the fried polenta (see page 68), after shaping it into a mound, leave to harden (or else use left-overs), cut into slices and then into sticks about 4-5 cm/2 in long. Fry in plenty of boiling oil until they are golden and crispy, drain and sprinkle with salt. Fried polenta is also excellent as a tasty appetiser or a delicious home-made snack.

"PEVERADA"

Liver and anchovy sauce

100 g/3 1/2 oz chicken livers	Parsley	Difficulty: ●●
120 g/4 oz Venetian soppressa (or lean salami)	Vinegar, Olive oil	Flavour: ●●●
		Kcal (per serving): 289
1 anchovy	Servings: 4	Proteins (per serving): 17
1 clove garlic	Preparation time: 20'	Fats (per serving): 24
1 lemon	Cooking time: 10'	Nutritional content: ●●●

1 Clean, wash and dry the chicken livers and chop them. Wash and fillet the anchovy.
In a frying-pan, sauté the garlic over a lively heat in 6-7 tablespoons of oil. When it begins to colour, remove and tip in the chicken livers, the chopped anchovy filet, the grated rind of half a lemon, a finely-chopped sprig of parsley and the soppressa (or salami), also chopped.

2 Season with salt and pepper, add a finger of vinegar and a few drops of lemon juice, and let the sauce reduce for a few minutes.
In Veneto *peverada* is the ideal accompaniment for meat, poultry and game, as we can see in the recipes in the relevant section.

Soppressa is a typical pork sausage of the Triveneto region, made with 65% lean meat and 35% fat, stuffed into a tube of the gut. If you can't find it, you can use chopped lean salami or seasoned sausage or, if you opt for a lighter version of peverada, *you can even leave it out altogether.*

"PEARÀ"

Meat and bread sauce

Beef marrow
1 1/2 pt/4 cups beef stock
300 g/11 oz stale home-
   made bread
Whole black peppercorns

Servings: 6	
Preparation time: 30'	
Cooking time: 2-3h	
Difficulty: ●●	
Flavour: ●●●	
Kcal (per serving): 254	
Proteins (per serving): 6	
Fats (per serving): 1	
Nutritional content: ●●●	

1 Grate the bread and tip it into a casserole. Pour in the stock a little at a time, mixing with an egg whisk.

2 Add the beef marrow and plenty of freshly-ground pepper, stirring all the time but without touching the bottom of the pan which should form a springy crust. The sauce should cook for at least two hours and, while taking care not to scrape the bottom of the pan, the longer it cooks the better it is. Serve hot, it should give off an inviting peppery fragrance.

Like pevarada, pearà *too is a ubiquitous presence on the tables of Verona; it is a splendid accompaniment to both white and red boiled meats.*

22

Pasta dishes and soups

2

"BIGOLI CO L'ANARA"

"Bigoli" with duck

500 g/1 lb 2 oz "bigoli"
(see below)
1 duck of about 1.2 kg/2¹/₂ lb
(complete with giblets)
1 carrot
1 onion
1 stalk celery
Sage
20 g/³/₄ oz butter
Olive oil
Grated Parmesan cheese
(optional)

Servings: 6	
Preparation time: 30'	
Cooking time: 1h 45'	
Difficulty: ●●	
Flavour: ●●●	
Kcal (per serving): 754	
Proteins (per serving): 49	
Fats (per serving): 29	
Nutritional content: ●●●	

1 The duck should be ready to cook, that is with the entrails removed (keeping aside the heart, liver, stomach etc), plucked, singed and washed. Boil it in a saucepan with the carrot, onion, celery and a pinch of salt for about an hour and a half.

2 Clean the giblets and chop them roughly: sauté for 4-5 minutes in a frying-pan with the butter, 2-3 tablespoons of oil and a sprig of sage, and season with salt and pepper. Cook the *bigoli* in the sieved and skimmed duck stock, and drain while they are still *al dente*. Serve with the giblet sauce, and sprinkled with Parmesan cheese if desired.

This delicious recipe comes from the Thiene area.
The bigoli *are traditionally prepared by hand, working together for about half an hour 500 g/1 lb 2 oz of flour, 2 eggs (preferably duck eggs), 40 g/1¹/₂ oz melted butter, and a glass of milk.*
The pastry is then passed through a special large-holed pasta press known as a bigolaro. *Once prepared the* bigoli *should be left to rest for at least one day, without letting them dry out.*
Alternatively, egg taglierini can be used.
A little tomato purée or conserve can be added to the giblet sauce. The duck itself can be eaten as a main course, served with baked artichokes (see p. 152) and, above all, with a fragrant peverada (see p. 20).

| 350 g/12 oz wholewheat "bigoli" |
| 100 g/3^1/$_2$ oz minced pork |
| 70 g/2^1/$_2$ oz minced veal |
| 1 carrot |
| 1 onion |
| 1 stalk celery |
| 350 g/12 oz peeled tomatoes |
| Nutmeg |
| Olive oil |
| Grated Parmesan cheese (optional) |

Servings:	4
Preparation time:	15'
Cooking time:	55'
Difficulty:	●●
Flavour:	●●●
Kcal (per serving):	714
Proteins (per serving):	31
Fats (per serving):	28
Nutritional content:	●●●

"BIGOLI COL TOCIO"

"Bigoli" with meat and tomato sauce

1 Place the minced meats in a casserole with the peeled tomatoes, a pinch of salt, a little grated nutmeg and half a glass of warm water. Bring to the boil slowly, and leave to simmer for about half an hour.

2 Peel and wash the vegetables, chop and sauté in a frying-pan in 5-6 tablespoons of oil. Tip in with the meat and cook, stirring all the time, for another quarter of an hour.

Cook the *bigoli* in plenty of boiling salted water, drain them while they are still *al dente* and serve with the sauce, sprinkling with grated cheese if you wish.

If you cannot find or make the bigoli, you can use wholewheat spaghetti or bucatini in both this and the following recipe.

25

"BIGOLI" IN SALSA

"Bigoli" in sauce

350 g/12 oz wholewheat
 "bigoli"
250 g/9 oz salted
 anchovies (or pilchards)
1 onion
Olive oil

Servings: 4	
Preparation time: 15′	
Cooking time: 55′	
Difficulty: ●●	
Flavour: ●●●	
Kcal (per serving): 655	
Proteins (per serving): 23	
Fats (per serving): 29	
Nutritional content: ●●●	

Wash the anchovies under cold running water, then fillet them, removing the heads and bones. Peel the onion, chop it finely and sauté in a frying-pan in 4-5 tablespoons of oil. Add the anchovy fillets and a little pepper (salt should not be necessary). At the same time, cook the *bigoli* in plenty of lightly salted water, and drain them before they are completely cooked. Tip them into the sauce and mix over the heat for a few minutes. Serve immediately. The addition of cheese is not recommended, but a trickle of olive oil will not go amiss.

400 g/14 oz dried cannellini (or haricot) beans
80 g/3 oz bacon fat or ham fat
Half a Savoy cabbage
1 onion
1 clove garlic
1 stalk celery
Parsley
Grated Parmesan xheese

Servings:	4
Preparation time:	15' + 4-5h
Cooking time:	1h 40'
Difficulty:	●●
Flavour:	●●●
Kcal (per serving):	589
Proteins (per serving):	29
Fats (per serving):	25
Nutritional content:	●●

"IOTA"

Cabbage and bean soup

The beans should be steeped for at least 4-5 hours in advance. Bring to the boil in plenty of unsalted water over a gentle heat and simmer until they are cooked al dente. Meanwhile dice the bacon and finely chop the onion, garlic and a sprig of parsley. Clean the cabbage and cut it into thin slices and chop the celery, then tip all the ingredients into the saucepan with the beans. Season with salt and pepper, and add more boiling water if necessary. Cover the saucepan, and cook over a very gentle heat for about an hour. Serve the iota generously sprinkled with grated Parmesan cheese.

This exquisite soup (also known as ota) originates from Carnia, but in Friuli and Venezia Giulia (especially in Gorizia and Trieste) it becomes a masterpiece. In this version we have used white cannellini or haricot beans, but it is also superb made with brown borlotti beans.

"BROÉTO"

Fish soup

1 Prepare and clean the fish. Cut off the heads of the mullet, gurnard and gudgeon (but don't throw them away) then wash the fish. Chop up the mullet, and boil it in a casserole in a little lightly salted water. Put all the other fish and the heads (including that of the mullet) into another casserole, cover with water and add a chopped sprig of parsley. Season with salt and bring to the boil.

2 After a quarter of an hour, remove the fish (including the mullet) with a fish slice, then cook the heads for another three-quarters of an hour. Keep the mullet stock hot in its casserole.

3 Remove the casserole with the fish heads from the heat, and pass the contents through a food mill (or the food processor) then tip it into the mullet stock.

A superb sunset over the Po delta.

		Servings: 8	Fats (per serving): 28
1 mullet (of about 1 kg/2¹/₄ lb)	1 carrot		Nutritional content: ●●
	1 onion, 1 stalk celery	Preparation time: 25'	
1 small gurnard	Parsley	Cooking time: 1h 20'	
1 small gudgeon	1 lemon	Difficulty: ●●●	
150 g/5 oz mixed soup fish	Slices of lightly-fried bread (to accompany)	Flavour: ●●●	
		Kcal (per serving): 516	
3 cloves garlic	Olive oil (or butter)	Proteins (per serving): 22	

4 Bone and skin all the fish except the mullet and whiz in the food processor, then tip into the casserole along with the pieces of mullet, mix well and allow the flavours to blend, then switch off the heat. Fry the slices of bread lightly in oil or butter, and place one in each soup bowl. Distribute the pieces of mullet between the dishes, ladle the creamy fish stock over them and serve.

CANNELLONI VICENTINI

Cannelloni, Vicenza style

1 Trim and wash the spinach and scald it with just the water that clings to the leaves. Drain, squeeze and chop it, and blend in a knob (10 g/^{1}/$_3$ oz) of melted butter. Sauté the minced meats and the tongue in a casserole in 20 g/^{2}/$_3$ oz of butter, and season with salt and pepper. Pour over half a glass of wine, and let it evaporate over a rapid heat. Remove from the heat, tip into a bowl and mix with the spinach.

2 Peel and chop the onion, then sauté in a saucepan with a finely-chopped sprig of parsley and 3-4 tablespoons of oil. Add the tomatoes, salt, pepper and a pinch of oregano, and reduce for about 20 minutes. Prepare the béchamel with 60 g/2 oz butter, 30 g/1 oz flour and the milk; let it thicken slowly, adding a pinch of grated nutmeg at the end.

3 Knead together 400 g/14 oz of flour with 4 eggs, a pinch of salt, a tablespoon of oil and enough water to obtain a soft, pliable dough. Roll into a ball and leave to rest briefly, then roll out thin and cut into rectangles of 12 cm by 8 (5 by 3 in). Cook in plenty of salted water, remove while still *al dente* and lay carefully to dry on a tea-towel.

4 Finely chop one bay leaf and two of sage, and a sprig each of basil and marjoram, then stir into the tomato sauce. Tip in the meat and spinach mixture, adding 4-5 tablespoons of Parmesan, a third of the béchamel, the two remaining eggs, and salt and pepper. Spread the filling in the centre of the pasta rectangles and roll them up. Set the *cannelloni* in a well-buttered oven-proof dish, cover with béchamel, sprinkle with the remaining Parmesan and dot with flakes of butter. Bake in a preheated oven at 190 °C for 20 minutes and serve.

450 g/1 lb flour	400 g/14 oz peeled	Dry white wine	Cooking time: 1h 20'
100 g/3¹/₂ oz minced pork	tomatoes	Grated Parmesan cheese	Difficulty: ●●●
150 g/5 oz minced veal	Onion, bay leaves, basil,	100 g/3¹/₂ oz butter	Flavour: ●●
100 g/3¹/₂ oz pickled	sage, marjoram,	Olive oil	Kcal (per serving): 952
tongue	oregano, parsley		Proteins (per serving): 44
6 eggs	7 dl/1¹/₂ pt/3 cups milk	Servings: 6-8	Fats (per serving): 53
200 g/7 oz spinach or chard	Nutmeg	Preparation time: 40' +15'	Nutritional content: ●●●

"CASUNZIEI" DI CORTINA

Cortina "casunziei"

300 g/11 oz flour
3 eggs
3 beetroot
2 potatoes
1 turnip
Breadcrumbs (if required)
Poppy seeds
Zigar cheese (or Parmesan)
50 g/2 oz butter

Servings: 4	
Preparation time: 40' + 15'	
Cooking time: 45'	
Difficulty: ●●●	
Flavour: ●●	
Kcal (per serving): 637	
Proteins (per serving): 22	
Fats (per serving): 22	
Nutritional content: ●●●	

Traditional costumes from the Belluno region.

1 Boil the beetroot, turnip and potatoes separately, peeling the potatoes while they are still hot. Grate the beetroot and turnip and mix them together in a bowl.

2 Mash the potatoes and mix them in with the other vegetables, adding a pinch of salt. If the mixture should be too moist, add a tablespoon of breadcrumbs.

3 On a floured work-surface, knead the flour with the eggs, a pinch of salt and enough warm water to obtain a firm dough. Form into a ball and leave to rest for a while, then roll out into a thin sheet and cut into squares of about 10 cm/4 in.

4 Place a ball of the filling in the centre of each square, then fold in two from corner to corner to make a triangle, pressing the edges tightly together with your fingertips. Cook the *casunziei* in moderately salted boiling water for about 10 minutes, removing them with a slatted spoon as they come to the surface. Serve with melted butter and sprinkled with grated zigar (a hard cheese from the Ampezzo region, which can be substituted with Parmesan or grana) and poppy seeds.

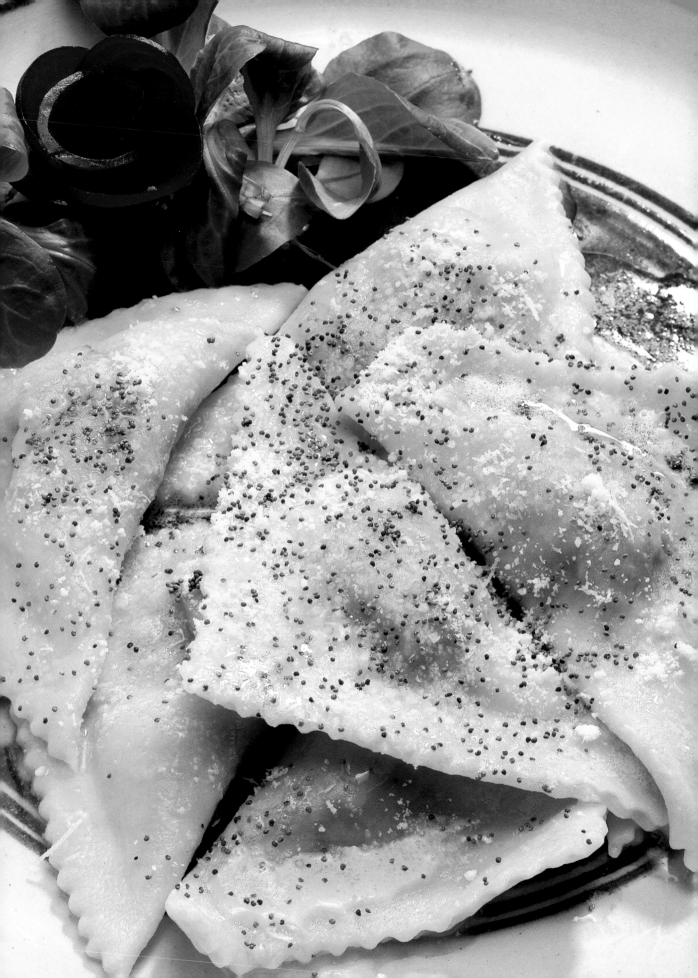

MINESTRA DI FAVE E SPECK

Speck and bean soup

450 g/1 lb shelled broad
    beans
200 g/7 oz speck
100 g/3¹/₂ oz ham
1 leek
350 g/12 oz tomatoes
Marjoram, parsley
1/2 l/1 pt/2 cups
    vegetable stock
Olive oil

Servings:	4-6
Preparation time:	15′
Cooking time:	1 h
Difficulty:	●●
Flavour:	●●●
Kcal (per serving):	590
Proteins (per serving):	23
Fats (per serving):	50
Nutritional content:	●●

Rinse the beans, put them into a saucepan and cover with lightly salted water. Scald for 4-5 minutes then drain and keep warm. Peel the leek and chop it up finely with the ham, a few sprigs of marjoram and one of parsley. Sauté in a casserole in 5-6 tablespoons of oil, then add the roughly-chopped tomatoes and season with salt and pepper. Leave to simmer for about ten minutes, then add the Speck cut into thin strips. Mix to blend the flavours, then add the vegetable stock. After about a quarter of an hour, add the broad beans and continue cooking for another half hour, adjusting salt and pepper to taste. Ladle the soup into individual soup bowls and let it cool slightly before serving.

You can use stock cubes, but the vegetable stock is actually very easy to make yourself (being light, it is perfect to add to dishes as they cook to maintain the cooking juices at the correct level). Take a carrot, an onion, a stalk of celery and a tomato and simmer for half an hour in a saucepan of lightly salted water.

"Mocnik" del Carso

Pasta soup

1 Mix a generous pinch of salt into the flour and pile in the centre of a floured work surface. Make a well in the middle and break in the egg, then beat it with a fork (or an egg-whisk) gradually incorporating the surrounding flour.

2 This will produce irregularly shaped lumps of dough, which you then work with your hands, blending in a little of the remaining flour to make them slightly larger.

200 g/7 oz flour
1 egg
60 g/2 oz butter

Servings: 4	
Preparation time: 20'	
Cooking time: 40'	
Difficulty: ●●	
Flavour: ●●	
Kcal (per serving): 324	
Proteins (per serving): 7	
Fats (per serving): 16	
Nutritional content: ●	

3 Melt the butter in a frying-pan and sauté the lumps of dough for 5-6 minutes. After this tip them, along with the remaining flour, into a saucepan with 2 litres/4 pints/8 cups of boiling, salted water. Cook for a good half hour, then ladle this cheap and simple soup from the Carso region into the individual soup bowls.

35

PASTA E "FASIOI"

Pasta and beans

500 g/1 lb 2 oz egg
  maltagliati (mixed
  shape flat soup pasta)
500 g/1 lb 2 oz borlotti
  beans
250 g/9 oz bacon rind
50 g/2 oz fat bacon
A piece of ham bone
1 onion
Cinnamon
Grated Parmesan cheese
  (optional)
Olive oil

Servings: 6	
Preparation time: 20' + 5-6h	
Cooking time: 2h	
Difficulty: ●●	
Flavour: ●●●	
Kcal (per serving): 881	
Proteins (per serving): 33	
Fats (per serving): 46	
Nutritional content: ●●●	

Set the beans to steep 5-6 hours in advance. Peel and chop the onion, then clean the bacon rind, scraping it well, and chop into thin strips. Drain the beans, and tip them into a casserole with about 2 litres/4 pints/8 cups of cold water, a drop of olive oil, the onion, a pinch of cinnamon, the bacon rind, the piece of ham bone and the chopped bacon. Season with salt and pepper.

Cover the casserole and set it over a fairly gentle heat, leaving to simmer as slowly as possible until the beans begin to disintegrate, making the stock rich and creamy.

Cook the maltagliati in plenty of boiling, salted water, and drain while they are still al dente. Serve the exquisite pasta and beans in individual dishes, trickling a little oil over each along with a generous twist of freshly-ground pepper.

"SOPA COADA"

Pigeon and bread terrine

Make sure that the pigeons are duly cleaned, plucked and singed. Peel and wash the vegetables, then chop them up small and sauté in a frying-pan over a gentle heat in 50 g/2 oz of melted butter and a half ladleful of stock. Brown the pigeons over a medium heat, pour over half a glass of wine and let it evaporate. Season with salt and pepper, lower the heat and leave to cook slowly for three quarters of an hour, adding a few more spoonfuls of stock if necessary. In the meantime cut the crusts off the slices of bread and fry them in the remaining butter, drain and keep warm.

Remove the pigeons from the saucepan and bone, then chop the flesh finely.
Arrange a layer of fried bread in the bottom of an ovenproof dish and sprinkle generously with stock. Over this spread a layer of pigeon meat sprinkled with Parmesan. Continue alternating layers in this way, ending with a layer of bread. Bake in a very low oven at a maximum of 100 °C, leaving the dish to *coàr* or "hatch" for at least 3 hours. If it should become too dry, add a little extra stock gradually, but with moderation. Bring to the table, and serve: delicious.

If you should happen to make too much, all to the good! Try it the next day re-heated very slightly in the oven. In terms of modern nutritional thinking, this succulent speciality is to be considered a meal in itself, accompanied with a green salad, and followed by a fruit or jam tart.

RAVIOLI DELLA VAL PUSTERIA

350 g/12 oz rye flour	40 g/1¹/₂ oz butter	Cooking time: 30'
700 g/1¹/₂ lb spinach	40 g/1¹/₂ oz lard	Difficulty: ●●●
Half an onion		Flavour: ●●
1 egg		Kcal (per serving): 816
3 dl/10 fl oz/ 1¹/₄ cups		Proteins (per serving): 66
milk	Servings: 4	Fats (per serving): 25
Cumin	Preparation time: 30' + 15'	Nutritional content: ●●●

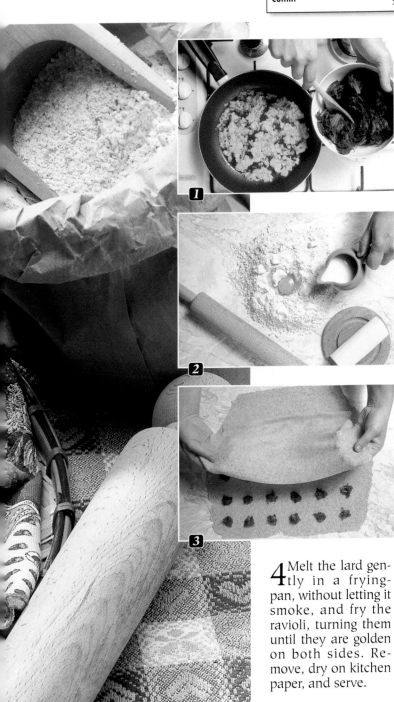

1 Trim and wash the spinach and scald it without adding any water except that which clings to the leaves. Drain, squeeze and chop it. In a frying-pan sauté the finely-chopped onion in 20 g/²/₃ oz of melted butter, and tip in the chopped spinach. Season with salt and sprinkle over a pinch of cumin; allow the flavours to blend, then remove from the heat.

2 Pile the flour in the centre of a floured work surface. Make a well in the centre and break in the egg, adding the remainder of the softened butter and a pinch of salt. Knead well, gradually incorporating enough warm milk to produce a smooth, pliable dough. Leave to rest briefly.

3 Roll out the dough thin into a large rectangle and cut in two. On one half arrange balls of the spinach mixture the size of a walnut at intervals of about 4-5 cm/1¹/₂-2 in. Cover with the other half and press down in the spaces between the filling. Cut out the ravioli with a pastry wheel.

4 Melt the lard gently in a frying-pan, without letting it smoke, and fry the ravioli, turning them until they are golden on both sides. Remove, dry on kitchen paper, and serve.

ZUPPA DI TRIPPE

Tripe soup

1 kg/2¹/4 lb tripe
1 calf's' foot (or bullock's)
120 g/4 oz bacon fat
1 carrot, 1 onion, 1 stalk
  celery
1 clove garlic
Parsley and rosemary
Slices of toasted home-
  made bread (to
  accompany)

Servings: 6	
Preparation time: 15'	
Cooking time: 3h 40'	
Difficulty: ●●	
Flavour: ●●●	
Kcal (per serving): 833	
Proteins (per serving): 45	
Fats (per serving): 53	
Nutritional content: ●●●	

1 Wash the tripe and put it in a saucepan. Cover with plenty of cold water and add the carrot, onion, celery and a sprig of parsley. Add the trimmed and cleaned calf's foot, season with salt, cover, and boil for 3 hours.

2 Remove the tripe and the calf's foot from the saucepan. Skim the stock and keep it warm. Bone the calf's foot and chop the meat and the drained tripe into pieces.

3 Dice the bacon fat small, and sauté lightly in a frying-pan with the garlic and rosemary and a trickle of water.

4 Tip the chopped veal and tripe back into the stock, add the bacon, adjust salt and boil for another half hour. Lay a slice of toasted bread in each soup bowl and ladle the soup over it.

ZUPPA FRIULANA

Friuli soup

400 g/14 oz valerian
1 leek
6-8 sausages
Vegetable stock (see p. 34)
Slices of rye bread (to
   accompany)
Olive oil

Servings:	4
Preparation time:	15'
Cooking time:	40'
Difficulty:	●●
Flavour:	●●●
Kcal (per serving):	763
Proteins (per serving):	34
Fats (per serving):	52
Nutritional content:	●●

Boil the sausages in plenty of water, drain and slice into rounds. Trim and wash the valerian, scalding it briefly in a little very lightly salted water.

Trim and wash the leek and cut into very fine disks. Sauté in a casserole in 4-5 tablespoons of oil, then add the roughly-chopped valerian. Let the flavours blend for 4-5 minutes, stirring all the time; add the sausages and leave to simmer over a gentle heat.

Pour in sufficient vegetable stock to cover the contents of the pan, season with salt and pepper, and simmer gently for another ten minutes. Switch off the heat and leave to cool slightly, then serve with slices of rye or wholemeal bread, which each diner can dip or break into the soup as he or she prefers.

RICE
AND RISOTTOS

3

L "RISI" CON LE QUAGLIE

Rice with quail

1 Clean and singe the quail, then wash and dry them. Put a pinch of salt and pepper in the stomach cavity, then lay two sage leaves on each, wrap in strips of bacon and tie up with kitchen string.

2 Chop the onion finely and sauté with the quail in an ovenproof dish in half the butter. As soon as the birds are nicely coloured all over, pour over half a glass of wine and let it evaporate. Cook in a pre-heated oven at

The sixteenth-century villa "la Rotonda" in Vicenza, one of Andrea Palladio's masterpieces.

		Cooking time: 45'
300 g/11 oz risotto rice	Grated Parmesan cheese	
4 quail	70 g/2¹/₂ oz butter	Difficulty: ●●
50 g/2 oz thinly-sliced bacon		Flavour: ●●
1 onion		Kcal (per serving): 650
Sage		Proteins (per serving): 20
Dry white wine	Servings: 4	Fats (per serving): 28
Vegetable stock (see p. 34)	Preparation time: 25'	Nutritional content: ●●●

180 °C for 25 minutes.

3 Cook the rice in a casserole in about 1 litre/2 pints/4 cups of lightly salted vegetable stock.

4 Drain the rice and transfer to a warm serving-dish. Add the remaining butter and the Parmesan, and blend in thoroughly. Trickle over the quail cooking juices, lay the birds on top of the rice (after removing the string) and serve.

3

4

"RISI COI PEOCI"

Rice with mussels

300 g/11 oz risotto rice
800 g/1³/4 lb mussels
150 g/5 oz shelled peas
2 cloves garlic
Parsley
Red chilli pepper
Olive oil

Servings: 4	
Preparation time: 20'	
Cooking time: 35'	
Difficulty: ●●	
Flavour: ●●●	
Kcal (per serving): 498	
Proteins (per serving): 16	
Fats (per serving): 17	
Nutritional content: ●●	

Wash the mussels, scraping them well and removing the "beard" which protrudes from the shells. Wash and dry a large sprig of parsley, peel the garlic and chop them up finely together then sauté half in a frying-pan in 3-4 tablespoons of oil. After a few moments tip in the mussels and let them open over a lively heat. Pour over half a ladleful of lightly salted water, lower the heat and let the flavours blend for about 5-6 minutes.

Take the mussels off the heat. Sieve the cooking juices and keep to one side. Remove the mussels from their shells and keep warm (without letting them cook fur-ther). Put the remainder of the chopped garlic and parsley into a casserole with 4-5 tablespoons of oil. Add the rice and roast it, stirring all the time, over a rapid heat. Add the peas, a pinch of salt, the crushed chilli pepper and a ladleful of the mussels' cooking juices diluted in hot water in a proportion of 1 to 4. Lower the heat and cook the risotto for about 20 minutes, adding more fish stock a little at a time as it becomes absorbed.

About 5 minutes before the rice is cooked, add the mussels and mix in gently. Serve the risotto hot but not boiling, garnishing the plates with sprigs of parsley.

"RISI E BISATI"

Rice and eels

1 Clean the eels (if they are small you don't need to skin them), wash and chop into pieces. Finely chop a sprig of parsley and sauté it lightly with the garlic in a casserole in 4-5 tablespoons of oil; remove the garlic when it begins to colour and tip the eel into the casserole.

2 Sauté for a few minutes, then add the bay leaf, a pinch of salt and the juice of one lemon. After 3-4 minutes add the rice, roasting it over a rapid heat for a couple of minutes and then adding a couple of ladlefuls of hot stock. Complete cooking, adding more hot stock gradually as required, and seasoning with salt and pepper to taste.

350 g/12 oz rice
2-3 small eels
2 cloves garlic
1 lemon
1 bay leaf
Parsley
Vegetable stock
    (see page 34)
Olive oil

Servings: 4	
Preparation time: 15'	
Cooking time: 35'	
Difficulty: ●●	
Flavour: ●●	
Kcal (per serving): 551	
Proteins (per serving): 15	
Fats (per serving): 23	
Nutritional content: ●●	

"RISI E BISI"

Rice and peas

180-200 g/6-7 oz soup rice
200 g/7 oz fresh shelled
   peas
80 g/3 oz bacon fat
1 onion
Parsley
Vegetable stock
   (see page 34)
Grated Parmesan cheese
   (optional)
Olive oil

Servings: 4	
Preparation time: 10'	
Cooking time: 30'	
Difficulty: ●●	
Flavour: ●●	
Kcal (per serving): 548	
Proteins (per serving): 10	
Fats (per serving): 33	
Nutritional content: ●●	

1 Dice or finely slice the bacon fat. Trim and peel the onion and slice it thinly, then sauté with the bacon fat in a casserole in 3-4 tablespoons of oil.

48

2 Wash the peas and tip them into the casserole without drying them, with a pinch of salt and pepper.

3 Cook over a rapid heat for about ten minutes, then pour in the warm stock and bring gently to the boil.

4 Add the rice, stirring every so often, and cook until it is *al dente*. Serve in individual bowls, letting it cool slightly and sprinkling with grated Parmesan, if desired, and finely-chopped parsley.

If we want to be true to the genuine Veneto tradition, instead of vegetable stock we use fresh peas in season, podding them ourselves and then boiling the pods for an hour in water, and using the resulting stock in the recipe.

49

"RISI IN CAVROMAN"

Rice with mutton

350 g/12 oz risotto rice
400 g/14 oz mutton
(preferably shoulder)
1 onion
300 g/11 oz peeled
tomatoes
Cinnamon
Vegetable stock
(see page 34)
Grated Parmesan cheese
(optional)
40 g/1¹/₂ oz butter

Servings: 4	
Preparation time: 15′	
Cooking time: 1h 30′	
Difficulty: ●●	
Flavour: ●●●	
Kcal (per serving): 738	
Proteins (per serving): 23	
Fats (per serving): 36	
Nutritional content: ●●●	

1 Wash the mutton, dry it and chop into pieces. Peel the onion and chop it up small, sauté lightly in melted butter in a casserole, then tip in the mutton chunks.

3 Leave the flavours to blend for a few minutes, then cover the meat with hot stock. Put the lid on the casserole and simmer for a good hour. Remove the mutton and bone it.

2 Brown the meat on both sides, season with salt and pepper and add the peeled and seeded tomatoes and a stick of cinnamon.

4 Put the boned meat back into the casserole and add the rice. Complete cooking, gradually adding further stock as required, and stirring all the time with a wooden spoon. Serve the rice hot, sprinkled with Parmesan cheese if you wish.

Flocks at pasture in the plain.

RISOTTO ALLA SBIRRAGLIA

Risotto with chicken and vegetables

300 g/11 oz risotto rice
400 g/14 oz hen or chicken breast
100 g/3¹/₂ oz bacon
1 carrot
1 white onion
1 stalk celery
1 ripe tomato
Stock (preferably beef and chicken)
Dry white wine
Grated Parmesan cheese
80 g/3 oz butter

Servings:	4
Preparation time:	25'
Cooking time:	45'
Difficulty:	●●
Flavour:	●●
Kcal (per serving):	866
Proteins (per serving):	23
Fats (per serving):	48
Nutritional content:	●●●

1 Wash the tomato, chop in half and seed it. Peel and wash the carrot and the celery and chop roughly. Clean the hen or chicken breast, removing the wishbone and cartilage if necessary. Peel the onion, chop it up small and sauté lightly in a casserole with the diced bacon in 50 g/2 oz of melted butter; add the carrots and celery and continue sautéing. After 5-6 minutes add the meat cut into thin slices and season with salt and pepper. Cover the casserole and let the flavours blend over a gentle heat. After ten minutes remove the lid, pour over half a glass of wine and let it evaporate.

2 Add the thinly-sliced tomato and, after 2-3 minutes, the rice, moistening with a ladleful of stock. Lower the heat and continue cooking the risotto for not more than 20 minutes, adding more stock gradually as it becomes absorbed. Switch off the heat, remove the carrot and celery and add the remaining butter and a generous handful of grated Parmesan. Cream this into the risotto for 3-4 minutes off the heat. Serve hot, but not boiling.

RISOTTO CON I FINOCCHI

Risotto with fennel

350 g/12 oz risotto rice
300 g/11 oz young fennel
    heads
1 onion
Grated Parmesan cheese
Vegetable stock
    (see page 34)
40 g/1¹/2 oz butter

Servings: 4	
Preparation time: 15′	
Cooking time: 25′	
Difficulty: ●●	
Flavour: ●●	
Kcal (per serving): 461	
Proteins (per serving): 10	
Fats (per serving): 12	
Nutritional content: ●●	

Wash the fennel and cut into pieces. Peel the onion and chop it finely, then sauté lightly in the melted butter in a casserole. Add the fennel and let the flavours blend briefly, stirring all the time. Add the rice and complete cooking over a medium-low heat, gradually adding the stock as it becomes absorbed. Sprinkle the risotto generously with Parmesan cheese and serve.

RISOTTO DI MARE

Seafood risotto

1 Wash the shellfish under cold running water, then remove the crabs and shrimps from their shells (keeping the heads and shells to one side), then chop the meat into evenly-sized pieces.

2 Place the heads and shells in a casserole with plenty of water and a pinch of salt; bring to the boil and simmer for about twenty minutes.

3 Meanwhile, peel the onion, cut it into thin slices and sauté in the melted butter in a frying-pan along with 3-4 tablespoons of oil. Add the shellfish meat and the whole squills and pour over a glass of wine.

4 Let the wine evaporate over a rapid heat, then tip in the rice. Complete the cooking of the rice over a medium heat, adding a little of the hot fish stock from time to time as required, and adjusting salt and pepper to taste. Cheese is not required.

350 g/12 oz risotto rice	Olive oil	Cooking time: 45'
2-3 spider crabs		Difficulty: ●●●
1 dozen shrimps		Flavour: ●●●
1 dozen squills		Kcal (per serving): 668
1 onion		Proteins (per serving): 29
Dry white wine	Servings: 4	Fats (per serving): 20
40 g/1¹/₂ oz butter	Preparation time: 25'	Nutritional content: ●●●

RISOTTO NERO

Black risotto

300 g/11 oz rice
400 g/14 oz cuttlefish and
    baby squid
2 cloves garlic
Dry white wine
Red chilli pepper
Vegetable stock (see page
    34)
Parsley
Olive oil

Servings: 4	
Preparation time: 10'	
Cooking time: 25'	
Difficulty: ●●	
Flavour: ●●●	
Kcal (per serving): 483	
Proteins (per serving): 19	
Fats (per serving): 17	
Nutritional content: ●●	

As is well-known, to give this risotto its fine black colour we need the cuttlefish ink. So, whether you clean them yourself or whether you get the fishmonger to do it, make sure that you retain a couple of the ink-sacs; two will be more than enough.

Clean and trim the molluscs, removing the bone from the cuttlefish and the heads and cartilage from the baby squid. Slice the flesh into rings and chop the tentacles up small. Peel the garlic and chop it up with a well-washed sprig of parsley. Sauté lightly in a casserole in 5-6 tablespoons of oil. Add the fish flesh, a pinch of salt and the chilli pepper crushed up small and stir briefly letting the flavours blend, then pour over half a glass of wine. Cover the casserole and cook over a very low heat for a quarter of an hour.

Add the rice, roast it, stirring with a wooden spoon, then add a ladleful of vegetable stock and the cuttlefish ink. Lower the heat and cook the risotto for about 20 minutes, adding more stock a little at a time as it becomes absorbed.

Serve the risotto hot, not boiling, garnishing the plates with sprigs of parsley.

Parmesan? Perish the thought!

POLENTA, GNOCCHI AND CANEDERLI

4

CANEDERLI DI FEGATO

Liver dumplings

1 Crumble the bread into a bowl, moisten with a glass of milk and mix in the finely-chopped liver, the flour and the semolina. Blend until you have a smooth, lump-free mixture.

2 Grate the lemon rind, chop the half onion and a sprig of parsley finely, and add to the mixture along with a pinch of grated nutmeg, salt and pepper. Mix well and leave to rest for about twenty minutes.

3 Break in the eggs and mix, then leave to rest for a further ten minutes.

4 Form the mixture into balls of about 4-5 centimetres/1^1/$_2$-2 inches diameter, then boil in a generous litre/2 pints/4 cups of beef stock for about 12 minutes. Distribute the canederli in individual bowls, with a little stock and a sprinkle of chopped chives.

300 g/11 oz/ calves' liver	Half a lemon	Servings: 4	Fats (per serving): 11
400 g/14 oz stale home-made bread (unsalted)	Milk	Preparation time: 40' + 30'	Nutritional content: ●●●
100 g/3¹/2 oz flour	Parsley	Cooking time: 12'	
50 g/2 oz semolina	Nutmeg	Difficulty: ●●	
2 eggs	Chives	Flavour: ●●	
Half an onion	Beef stock	Kcal (per serving): 611	
		Proteins (per serving): 34	

The canederli (the Italian name for the German knödeln) are also excellent sprinkled with breadcrumbs and dotted with butter or melting cheese and baked in a hot oven for 10 minutes. They can be served on their own or as an accompaniment to a stew or goulash, (although when used as an accompaniment the dumplings should preferably be made without meat and with 4 eggs in the mixture). There are many other different types of canederli, such as those made with salami or lucanica, the typical Veneto sausage, with spinach, with cow's or goat's milk, or the canederli de poìna made with ricotta, the recipe for which follows.

59

400 g/14 oz ricotta
4 eggs
30 g/1 oz flour
Breadcrumbs
Asiago d'allevo cheese (or
    grated Parmesan)
30 g/1 oz butter

Servings: 4	
Preparation time: 40' + 15'	
Cooking time: 10'	
Difficulty: ●●	
Flavour: ●●	
Kcal (per serving): 621	
Proteins (per serving): 25	
Fats (per serving): 47	
Nutritional content: ●●●	

CANEDERLI "DE POÌNA"

Dumplings with ricotta

As well as being fresh, the ricotta should also be fairly firm, since this influences not only the quality but also the consistency of these delicious gnocchi. Delicately fold in the flour, the eggs, a generous handful of cheese and a pinch of salt, then add sufficient breadcrumbs to produce a fairly stiff mixture, which you should then leave to rest briefly. Shape into balls and then cook the canederli for 8-10 minutes in a saucepan of hot, but not boiling, water. Drain, and serve with butter and plenty of grated cheese.

Asiago is one of the most versatile and popular cheeses of Trentino and Veneto. The d'allevo variety (of a compact consistency) can, depending on how mature it is, be used either for normal consumption or for grating, while the pressato variety is used exclusively for grating. If you can't get hold of Asiago you can use Parmesan or grana instead.

"CIARONCIÈ" DI MOENA

Spinach-filled potato pasta

1 Boil the potatoes and peel them while they are still hot, then mash or purée them and leave to cool. Fold in the flour and the egg, then knead, adding another egg if the dough is not firm enough. Roll out the dough thin like pastry with a rolling-pin, then cut out squares of about 10 cm/4 in with a pastry wheel.

2 Trim, wash and scald the spinach (traditionally wild spinach is used) using only the water which clings to the leaves, then drain and squeeze it. Chop finely and sauté briefly in a frying-pan in 30 g/1 oz melted butter with a pinch of salt. Place a teaspoon of spinach in the centre of each pastry square, then fold it in two, and press the edges down well. Cook the *ciaronciè* in the remaining melted butter along with 3-4 tablespoons of oil. Serve them piping hot sprinkled with cheese.

500 g/1 lb 2oz potatoes
50 g/2 oz flour
1 egg
400 g/14 oz spinach
Grated Parmesan or grana cheese
80 g/3 oz butter

Servings:	4
Preparation time:	40'
Cooking time:	15'
Difficulty:	●●
Flavour:	●●
Kcal (per serving):	526
Proteins (per serving):	40
Fats (per serving):	23
Nutritional content:	●●

GNOCCHI

600 g/1¹/₄ lb potatoes
100 g/3¹/₂ oz flour (plus flour for rolling-out)
1 egg
Grated Parmesan cheese
40 g/1¹/₂ oz butter

Servings: 4	
Preparation time: 40'	
Cooking time: 10'	
Difficulty: ●●	
Flavour: ●●	
Kcal (per serving): 412	
Proteins (per serving): 15	
Fats (per serving): 17	
Nutritional content: ●●	

1 Boil the potatoes and peel them hot. Mash or purée them and leave to cool, then blend in the flour and the egg.

2 Knead to a soft, smooth dough, then divide into pieces and roll out with your hands on a well-floured work surface into long sausages about the width of a finger and 40 cm/16 in long.

Verona is the city which boasts the title of "Queen of the gnocchi". This traditional dish is an essential element of the Good Friday meal in the city of the Scaligers. In the district of San Zeno the day is traditionally celebrated by a procession in fifteenth-century costume which terminates with the nomination of the "Father of the Gnocco".

3 Chop into lengths of about 2 cm/³/₄ in; make a small well with the tip of your middle finger in the centre of each cylinder.

4 Bring a large saucepan of salted water to the boil and drop in the gnocchi a few at a time. As soon as they come to the surface remove with a fish-slice, drain, and place in a serving-dish. Garnish with plenty of butter and grated Parmesan.

GNOCCHETTI DI MILZA

Spleen gnocchetti

1 calf's spleen
2 eggs
1 carrot
1 stalk celery
1 clove garlic
Breadcrumbs
Parsley
Nutmeg
Beef or chicken stock
30 g/1 oz butter

Servings:	4
Preparation time:	30' + 15'
Cooking time:	10'
Difficulty:	●●
Flavour:	●●
Kcal (per serving):	309
Proteins (per serving):	25
Fats (per serving):	5
Nutritional content:	●●

1 Skin the spleen and patiently press out of the fibrous sac using the back of a stout kitchen knife. Chop the carrot, celery and garlic very fine, tip into a bowl with the spleen, the melted butter and the beaten eggs, add a pinch each of salt, pepper and nutmeg and mix thoroughly. Finally blend in enough breadcrumbs to produce a smooth, firm paste, which you should then leave to rest for a short time.

2 Shape into small gnocchi little bigger than a walnut. Cook them in the moderately salted boiling stock to which you have added a handful of chopped parsley. Switch off the heat after 5-6 minutes and serve the gnocchi in their broth in the individual soup bowls. Grated cheese can be used or not as preferred.

500 g/1 lb 2 oz potatoes
400 g/14 oz fresh plums
100 g/3^{1}/2 oz flour
1 egg
Granulated sugar and sugar lumps
Cinnamon
Sage
60 g/2 oz butter

Servings: 4	
Preparation time: 30' + 15'	
Cooking time: 10'	
Difficulty: ●●	
Flavour: ●●	
Kcal (per serving): 520	
Proteins (per serving): 12	
Fats (per serving): 18	
Nutritional content: ●●	

GNOCCHI DI PRUGNE

Plum gnocchi

Boil the potatoes and peel them hot. Mash or purée them and leave to cool, then blend in the flour 20 g/^{2}/3 oz of butter in flakes and the egg (add another egg if the dough should not be firm enough). Leave to rest briefly.

Wash the plums. Split them open and remove the stone, replacing it with half a sugar lump, then close up again and cover with a layer of dough, not too thin, shaping with your hands into the form of a large gnocco. Repeat this operation until all the ingredients are used up, then drop the gnocchi one at a time into a large saucepan of lightly salted boiling water over a medium heat. After 5-6 minutes remove the gnocchi one by one with a slatted spoon and drain well. Dip them swiftly into a bowl of sugar mixed with powdered cinnamon (you can also add chopped almonds or hazelnuts if you wish), then melt the remaining butter in a frying-pan with a leaf of sage and pour over the gnocchi.

GNOCCHI DI BOLZANO

100 g/3¹/₂ oz stale
   wholemeal bread
170 g/6 oz flour
2 eggs
40 g/1¹/₂ oz bacon fat
   (one slice)
40 g/1¹/₂ oz lean bacon
   (one slice)
40 g/1¹/₂ oz Speck
   (one slice)
Grated Parmesan cheese
Parsley
40 g/1¹/₂ oz butter
Olive oil

Servings: 4	
Preparation time: 30' + 15'	
Cooking time: 30'	
Difficulty: ●●	
Flavour: ●●●	
Kcal (per serving): 719	
Proteins (per serving): 18	
Fats (per serving): 48	
Nutritional content: ●●●	

1 Dice half the bread into evenly-sized cubes and grate the other half. Sauté briefly the chopped bacon fat, bacon and Speck in a casserole in a tablespoon of oil, then lightly fry the cubes of bread.

1

2

2 Place the flour in the middle of a floured work surface, then blend in the lightly fried bread cubes, bacon fat, bacon and Speck, the grated breadcrumbs, the eggs, a handful of Parmesan, a finely-chopped sprig of parsley and a pinch of salt. Mix thoroughly until you have a mixture of a fairly firm consistency, then leave to rest briefly.

3 Bring a large saucepan of lightly salted water to the boil and drop in spoonfuls of the mixture one at a time. Cook the gnocchi for a good twenty minutes, then remove them individually with a slatted spoon, and serve with melted butter and plenty of grated Parmesan cheese.

3

GNOCCHI CON LE "BRISE"

Gnocchi with porcini mushrooms

1 Grate the rolls into a bowl, and mix them with the beaten eggs, a glass of milk and a pinch of salt, then leave to rest for a couple of hours. Clean the mushrooms using a damp cloth without washing them, then chop them up roughly and not too small. Sauté them in a frying-pan in 2-3 tablespoons of oil, with the finely-chopped garlic and a pinch of salt.

2 Leave the mushrooms to cool, then add them to the contents of the bowl, along with a handful of

chopped parsley and 2 tablespoons of Parmesan. If the mixture is not stiff enough, add a tablespoon or two of flour. Bring a large saucepan of vegetable stock to the boil and drop in spoonfuls of the mushroom mixture. After 6-8 minutes begin to remove the gnocchi one by one with a slatted spoon. Drain well, and set in an ovenproof dish. Dot with flakes of butter, sprinkle with Parmesan and brown in a pre-heated oven at 200 °C for 5 minutes.

4 fairly stale rolls
300 g/11 oz Porcini
   mushrooms
2 eggs
1 clove garlic
20 g/^{2}/$_3$ oz flour
Milk
Parsley
Grated Parmesan cheese
Vegetable stock (see p. 34)
40 g/1^1/$_2$ oz butter
Olive oil

Servings: 4	
Preparation time: 30' + 2h	
Cooking time: 25'	
Difficulty: ●●	
Flavour: ●●	
Kcal (per serving): 575	
Proteins (per serving): 21	
Fats (per serving): 29	
Nutritional content: ●●	

67

POLENTA

500 g/1 lb 2 oz cornmeal
Servings: 4
Preparation time: 5'
Cooking time: 50'
Difficulty: ●●
Flavour: ●●
Kcal (per serving): 480
Proteins (per serving): 11
Fats (per serving): 4
Nutritional content: ●●

Ideally the polenta should be cooked in a copper saucepan, but a large, heavy-bottomed steel saucepan will do just as well.

Fill with about 2 litres/4 pints/8 cups of water and set over a rapid heat. As soon as it begins to boil add the cornmeal, sprinkling it in a little at a time and stirring constantly with a wooden spoon to avoid lumps forming,

After about three-quarters of an hour – when it begins to detach itself from the sides of the pan and it becomes increasingly difficult to stir – the polenta is cooked.

Tip it out onto a wooden chopping-board and cover with a clean tea-cloth. Bring it to the table on the board, along with the wire traditionally used to slice it.

The precise amount of water necessary for cooking the polenta actually depends on the quality and moisture content of the cornmeal, as well as on the strength of the cooking heat (the calories produced by the traditional fireplace are not comparable with those of a gas hob).

If you should need to add more water during cooking because the polenta becomes too dry – although this should not happen – make sure that it is hot. The long cooking of the cornmeal makes it highly digestible. Once cooked it can be kept for several days, and enjoyed either grilled or fried.

Polenta holds pride of place in the gastronomy of the Triveneto region, having fed innumerable generations of farmers, fishermen, shepherds and woodcutters. As we shall see further on in this book, it is also the ideal accompaniment for both sophisticated and simple dishes of meat and fish.

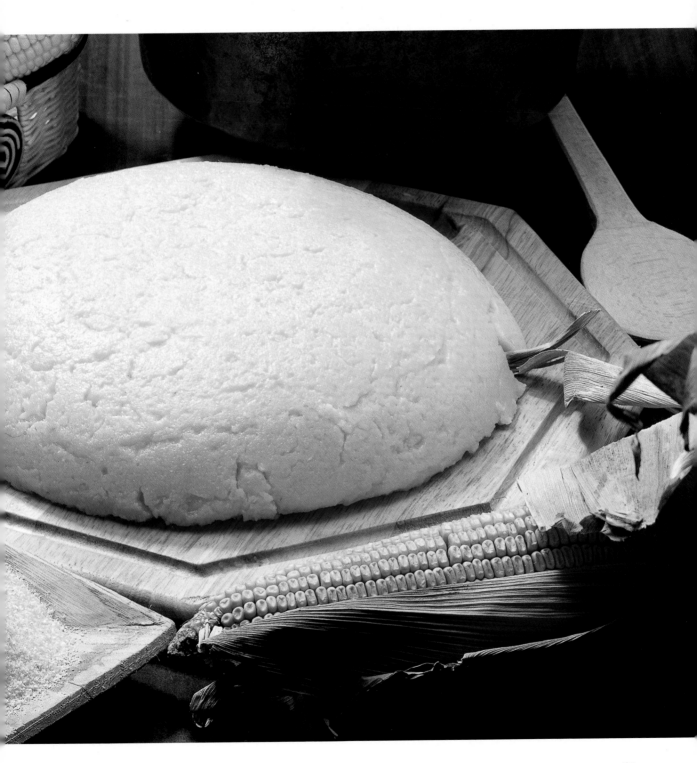

"POENTA PASTIZADA"

Baked polenta with meat and mushroom sauce

500 g/1 lb 2 oz cornmeal
300 g/11 oz loin of veal
(sliced)
100 g/3¹/₂ oz bacon
100 g/3¹/₂ oz chicken
hearts and livers
50 g/2 oz dried mushrooms
1 carrot, 1 onion, 1 stalk
celery
Tomato concentrate
Parsley
White wine
100 g/3¹/₂ oz grated
Parmesan cheese
140 g/5 oz butter

Servings: 6	
Preparation time: 25′ + 30′	
Cooking time: 1h 30′	
Difficulty: ●●●	
Flavour: ●●●	
Kcal (per serving): 760	
Proteins (per serving): 30	
Fats (per serving): 40	
Nutritional content: ●●●	

1 Steep the mushrooms in cold water for half an hour in advance. Trim the hearts and livers and wash them under cold running water; dry and put aside. Trim and peel the carrot, onion and celery and chop them up fine with a sprig of parsley and the bacon, then sauté lightly in a casserole in 30 g/1 oz of melted butter. Add the veal slices cut into thin strips, stirring them until they are nicely coloured then pour over half a glass of white wine.

2 Let this evaporate over a rapid heat, then add a tablespoon of tomato concentrate and two ladlefuls of hot water (alternatively you can use 200 g/7 oz of tomato purée), adjust salt to taste and cook over a moderate heat for ten minutes. Squeeze out the mushrooms, add them to the sauce and cook for another scant 10 minutes. Meanwhile sauté the chopped hearts and livers in 30 g/1 oz of melted butter in another small saucepan.

3 Prepare the polenta (see p. 68) without letting it become too stiff. Arrange a layer in the bottom of an ovenproof dish and spread a little of the meat and mushroom mixture over it, then sprinkle with Parmesan.

4 On top of this place another layer of polenta dribbled with 40 g/1$^{1}/_{2}$ oz melted butter, then sprinkle with Parmesan and scatter over it the sautéed hearts and livers. Follow this with another layer of polenta, spread with the rest of the meat and mushroom sauce and again sprinkled with Parmesan. Finish up with a layer of polenta dribbled with the remaining melted butter, and sprinkled with all the Parmesan you have left.

The polenta must be served piping hot, so we advise you to heat it up for a couple of minutes in a pre-heated oven at 200 °C before serving. Delicious.

POLENTA DI GRANO SARACENO

Buckwheat polenta

300 g/11 oz buckwheat
    flour
4-5 fresh anchovies
Grated cheese (Asiago
    d'allevo or Parmesan)
30 g/1 oz butter

Servings: 4	
Preparation time: 5'	
Cooking time: 50' + 15'	
Difficulty: ●●	
Flavour: ●●	
Kcal (per serving): 464	
Proteins (per serving): 20	
Fats (per serving): 17	
Nutritional content: ●●	

1 Wash, clean and fillet the anchovies, removing the heads and bones. Set the water to boil and cook the polenta (following the instructions on p. 68) for about 50 minutes, finishing up with a fairly stiff consistency, then tip into a well-buttered ovenproof dish.

2 Arrange the anchovy fillets over the top, and sprinkle with grated cheese. Brown in a pre-heated oven at 180 °C for about 15 minutes.

In the Trento area it is the custom to serve buckwheat polenta accompanied with boiled turnip leaves dressed with vinegar or lemon juice. Alternatively, it is also frequently served with Treviso radicchio cooked under the grill and seasoned with salt and olive oil.

MEAT

5

ANATRA RIPIENA

Stuffed duck

1 duck (1.5 kg/3¹/₄ lb)
200 g/7 oz minced veal
200 g/7 oz minced pork
1 egg
80 g/3 oz bacon fat (thinly
    sliced)
Breadcrumbs
Oregano, thyme
Vegetable stock (see p. 34)
Grated Parmesan cheese
60 g/2 oz butter

Servings:	4-6
Preparation time:	30'
Cooking time:	about 50'
Difficulty:	●●●
Flavour:	●●●
Kcal (per serving):	722
Proteins (per serving):	64
Fats (per serving):	45
Nutritional content:	●●●

1 Prepare the plucked duck for cooking, removing the innards (keep the liver aside), the head and neck, the feet and the wing-tips (making sure the fat gland has been removed). Singe and then wash and dry. Chop the liver and mix it in with the minced veal and pork, 2-3 tablespoons of Parmesan, a handful of breadcrumbs, oregano and thyme leaves, the egg, salt and pepper.

2 Stuff the duck with this filling, close up the flaps of the stomach cavity and sew up with kitchen thread. Rub the duck with butter, wrap it up in the strips of bacon fat, tie with kitchen string and set in a buttered ovenproof dish. Cook in a pre-heated oven at 180 °C for 45 minutes, basting with hot stock if necessary. Remove the string and serve fragrant and hot.

"SGUAZETO ALA BECHÉRA"

Braised lamb

Peel the onion and chop it up fine, then sauté in three or four tablespoons of oil in a casserole with the squashed garlic clove. Add the diced bacon and brown lightly over a moderate heat for 2-3 minutes. Add the lamb chopped into fairly large chunks and season with salt, pepper and a pinch of cinnamon. Dilute a tablespoon of tomato concentrate in a ladleful of stock and pour over.

Put the lid on the casserole and cook over a fairly gentle heat for about an hour, making sure that the sauce reduces sufficiently during the last few minutes.

The *sguazeto* should be served with polenta, preferably after a brief re-heating in the oven.

1 kg/2¹/4 lb shoulder of lamb
1 clove garlic
1 onion
100 g/3¹/2 oz bacon
Powdered cinnamon
Tomato concentrate
Vegetable stock (see p. 34)
Olive oil

Servings: 4	
Preparation time: 10′	
Cooking time: 1h 10′	
Difficulty: ●	
Flavour: ●●	
Kcal (per serving): 492	
Proteins (per serving): 31	
Fats (per serving): 37	
Nutritional content: ●●	

CONIGLIO ALLA TRENTINA

Rabbit, Trentino style

1 Half an hour in advance set a bay leaf, a few juniper berries and rosemary leaves, some cumin seeds and a pinch of nutmeg to steep in half a glass of wine. Prepare the rabbit for cooking, and cut it into pieces (keeping the liver aside). Peel and chop the onion and sauté in a frying-pan along with the chopped bacon fat in 4-5 tablespoons of oil and a knob of butter; tip in the rabbit pieces and brown gently.

2 Pour over a glass of wine and before it has evaporated completely pour in the mixture of herbs and spices macerated in the wine.

3 Leave to simmer as gently as possible, adding a ladleful of stock if and when necessary. In the meantime, chop the onion, carrot and a sprig of parsley finely and sauté lightly in a small saucepan in 2-3 tablespoons of oil. Add the chopped rabbit liver and brown gently. Mix in a tablespoon of tomato purée and one of flour diluted in a little stock, and thicken the sauce slowly, stirring all the time.

4 When the rabbit has cooked for three-quarters of an hour over a fairly gentle heat, pour in the vegetable, liver and tomato sauce, and cook, still over a gentle heat, for another three-quarters of an hour.

1 rabbit (about 1.3 kg/3 lb)	Cumin, nutmeg, bay leaf, juniper berries, rosemary	30 g/1 oz butter Olive oil	**Cooking time:** 1h 40'
60 g/2 oz bacon fat	Parsley		**Difficulty:** ●●
One and a half onions	Vegetable stock		**Flavour:** ●●
Half a carrot	(see p. 34)	**Servings:** 4	**Kcal (per serving):** 698
Tomato purée	Dry white wine		**Proteins (per serving):** 51
Flour		**Preparation time:** 15' + 30'	**Fats (per serving):** 41
			Nutritional content: ●●●

FEGATO ALLA VENEZIANA

Liver, Venetian style

700 g/1¹/₂ lb calves' liver
   (cut into thin slices)
3 onions
Olive oil
30g/1 oz butter
Parsley

Servings: 4	
Preparation time: 10'	
Cooking time: about 30'	
Difficulty: ●	
Flavour: ●●	
Kcal (per serving): 268	
Proteins (per serving): 25	
Fats (per serving): 17	
Nutritional content: ●	

Heat 8 tablespoons of oil in a large frying-pan and cook the thinly sliced onions slowly, stirring all the time, for about twenty minutes until they are a nice golden colour. Remove from the pan and keep warm. Add more oil and turn up the heat, then cook the liver cut into strips for a maximum of 5 minutes. Season with salt and pepper and tip the onions back into the pan.

Cook for another two minutes, stirring vigorously, then spoon onto a warm serving-dish. Melt the butter in the same frying-pan where you have cooked the liver and onions, gathering up the cooking juices with a wooden spoon and blending them thoroughly with the melted butter. Remove from the heat and add the chopped parsley, then pour the sauce over the liver.

| 600 g/1¼ lb calves' liver (in a single piece) |
| 1 carrot |
| 1 onion |
| 1 stalk celery |
| 1 lemon |
| Breadcrumbs |
| Parsley |
| 1 clove |
| Slices of toasted bread (for serving) |
| Olive oil |

Servings:	4
Preparation time:	20'
Cooking time:	2h 10'
Difficulty:	●●
Flavour:	●●
Kcal (per serving):	518
Proteins (per serving):	37
Fats (per serving):	18
Nutritional content:	●●

FEGATO ALLA TRIESTINA

Liver, Trieste style

1 Peel the liver, if necessary, then wash and dry it and stick the clove into it. Peel and chop onion, carrot and celery, and place in a casserole with 4-5 tablespoons of oil, 2 tablespoons of breadcrumbs and a sprig of parsley. Lay the liver on top and season with salt and pepper. Cover with cold water, put the lid on the casserole and set on the heat.

2 When it comes to the boil, remove the lid from the casserole, lower the heat to the minimum, and leave to simmer for a couple of hours, turning the liver from time to time. When cooking is complete the liver will be extraordinarily tender; cut it into thin slices and arrange these on a serving-dish with slices of toasted bread moistened slightly with the cooking juices. Squeeze over a little lemon juice, garnish with sprigs of parsley and serve.

1

2

CAPRIOLO ALLA MONTANARA

Roebuck, mountain style

1 Set the roebuck in a bowl with the sliced onion, the garlic, 3-4 cloves, salt, 2-3 tablespoons of oil and 4 of vinegar. Cover and leave to marinate for two or even three days, turning the meat over at least once a day.

2 Remove the meat from the marinade and drain. Sauté the diced bacon fat in a casserole over a lively heat in 2-3 tablespoons of oil, then put in the meat and brown it gently.

3 Pour over a glass of wine, a cup of stock and a generous glass of filtered marinade. Cover the casserole and leave to cook gently for a good hour. When cooked, remove the meat from the casserole and keep warm.

Monte Cristallo, one of the superb peaks of the Ampezzo Dolomites.

800 g/1³/4 lb roebuck meat (in a single piece)	Cloves	Olive oil	**Cooking time: 1h 15'**
50 g/2 oz bacon fat	Vinegar		**Difficulty: ●●**
1 onion	Vegetable stock (see p. 34)		**Flavour: ●●●**
1 clove garlic	Boiled potatoes (to accompany)		**Kcal (per serving): 809**
Cooking cream	Dry white wine	**Servings: 4**	**Proteins (per serving): 43**
		Prep. time: 20'+ 48-72h	**Fats (per serving): 49**
			Nutritional content: ●●●

4 Over a gentle heat, dilute the cooking juices in the casserole with a little filtered marinade, then tip in a glass of cream. Serve the roebuck with the sauce and boiled potatoes dotted with butter and sprinkled with salt. As well as roebuck, other types of furred game such as hare and wild boar can be prepared in the same way.

"LIÈVARO GARBO E DOLCE"

Sweet hare casserole

1 Wash and dry the skinned hare, then chop it into pieces (keeping the liver to one side). Place in a bowl, cover with red wine, add a few bay leaves and cloves and leave to marinate for 5-6 hours.

2 Peel and chop the onion, then sauté it with the chopped bacon fat in the melted butter in a casserole (preferably earthenware). Add the drained hare pieces and brown them well, then pour over the filtered marinade.

3 Cook gently for about an hour, then add the grated lemon peel, a pinch of cinnamon and a teaspoon of sugar. If you wish to add salt, do so in moderation so as not to spoil the delicate balance of the flavours.

1 well-hung hare of about 1.3 kg/3 lb (with liver)	Bay leaves	Servings: 4	Fats (per serving): 56
100 g/3 1/2 oz bacon fat	Cinnamon	Preparation time: 20' + 5-6h	Nutritional content: ●●●
1 onion	Cloves	Cooking time: 1h 50'	
1 lemon	Sugar	Difficulty: ●●	
20 g/2/3 oz raisins	Red wine	Flavour: ●●	
20 g/2/3 oz pine kernels	50 g/2 oz butter	Kcal (per serving): 801	
		Proteins (per serving): 40	

4 Let the flavours blend, then add the sliced liver, the raisins and the pine kernels, and complete cooking by leaving to simmer over a gentle heat for about half an hour.

LINGUA IN SALSA

Tongue in sauce

1 calf's tongue (about
   8-900 g/2 lb)
3-4 anchovies
Capers
Flour
Vegetable stock (see p. 34)
Dry white wine
40 g/1 1/2 oz butter

Servings:	4
Preparation time:	30'
Cooking time:	1h 30'
Difficulty:	●●●
Flavour:	●●●
Kcal (per serving):	697
Proteins (per serving):	49
Fats (per serving):	44
Nutritional content:	●●●

1 Singe the tongue briefly, as you would with a chicken, then beat it lightly on all sides to tenderise it.

2 When it is pliable, wash it under cold running water and remove the grey-coloured outer layer. Set in a casserole, cover with lightly salted water, put the lid on and place on the heat.

3 Boil for 40 minutes over a medium heat, then remove the tongue from the stock, and peel off the second, white-coloured layer. Coat lightly in flour and brown on all sides in the butter in a casserole, and complete cooking slowly, adding a little vegetable stock from time to time if necessary.

4 Meanwhile, trim, wash and fillet the anchovies and put them into a small saucepan with a tablespoon of capers and a glass of white wine. Boil for 5-6 minutes, then whiz the solid ingredients in the food processor and tip the purée back into the liquid. Blend over a gentle heat for 4-5 minutes. Serve the tongue warm, sliced and with the sauce spooned over it.

Venice, gondolas on the Grand Canal.

MAIALE AL LATTE ▸

Pork in milk

1 kg/2¹/₄ lb boned loin of
   pork
³/₄ litre/1¹/₄ pt/3 cups
   milk
A bunch of marjoram,
   rosemary and sage, tied
   together
Nutmeg
Dry white wine
60 g/2 oz butter

Servings: 4	
Preparation time: 20' + 24h	
Cooking time: 1h 40'	
Difficulty:	●●
Flavour:	●●
Kcal (per serving): 597	
Proteins (per serving): 49	
Fats (per serving): 32	
Nutritional content:	●●

1 Tie up the pork loin with string to keep it in shape, set it in a bowl with the bunch of herbs, cover with wine and leave to marinate for an entire day.

2 Drain the meat and brown it in the melted butter in a casserole, turning so that it becomes evenly-coloured on all sides. Season with a pinch of salt and one of nutmeg, then pour over the warm milk. Cover the casserole and leave to simmer over a very gentle heat for a generous one and a half hours. Cut into not too thick slices, arrange on a serving-dish and pour over the finely-sieved sauce.

STINCO AL FORNO

Roast shin of pork

Singe the shins, then wash and dry them. Make small slits with a knife and spike with slices of garlic and rosemary leaves, then brown on all sides in an ovenproof dish in the butter. Season with salt and pepper and pour over a glass of wine. When this has evaporated, set the dish in a pre-heated oven at 180 °C and cook for ¹/2 hours, basting from time to time with a little vegetable stock. Serve piping hot, with polenta. Veal shins can be prepared in the same way.

2 shins of pork 1.3 kg/3 lb	Rosemary	Servings: 4	Kcal (per serving): 473
2 cloves garlic	Dry white wine	Preparation time: 15'	Proteins (per serving): 42
Vegetable stock	60 g/2 oz butter	Cooking time: 1h 40'	Fats (per serving): 26
(see p. 34)		Difficulty: ●●	Nutritional content: ●●
		Flavour: ●●●	

"MÀSARO ALA VALESANA"

Mallard

1 Prepare the plucked mallard for cooking. Remove the innards, head and neck, the feet and the wing-tips (making sure the fat gland has been removed). Singe and then wash and dry. Place it in a deep bowl with sprigs of thyme and oregano, cover with vinegar and leave to marinate for at least 12 hours.

2 Remove the fowl from the marinade and drain. Put a pinch of salt and pepper in the stomach cavity, then rub the bird with butter and wrap it up in the strips of bacon fat, securing them if necessary with kitchen string. Set in a buttered ovenproof dish, and cook in a pre-heated oven at 180 °C for 15-20 minutes. Remove from the oven and cut into pieces.

3 Meanwhile clean, wash and fillet the anchovies. Peel and chop the onions and sauté lightly in 40 g/1^{1}/$_{2}$ oz of butter in a large frying-pan with the anchovy fillets and a tablespoon of capers.

4 After 3-4 minutes add the mallard pieces, brown well all over and season with salt and pepper. Pour over a glass of wine and complete cooking over a gentle heat (about 40 minutes in all).

		Servings: 4	Fats (per serving): 53
1 mallard (wild duck) of about 1.3 kg/3 lb	Oregano, thyme Vinegar	Preparation time: 30′ + 12h	Nutritional content: ●●●
80 g/3 oz bacon fat (thinly sliced)	1 glass dry white wine	Cooking time: 1h	
2 small onions	120 g/4 oz butter	Difficulty: ●●	
2 anchovies		Flavour: ●●●	
Capers		Kcal (per serving): 794	
		Proteins (per serving): 56	

Màsaro *is the Venetian name for the mallard, and* ala valesana *means that it is cooked in the traditional manner of the valley-dwellers. The reference here is not to mountain valleys but rather to the* valli *or fish-ponds, enclosed sections of the lagoon which were – at least in the past - densely populated with water fowl, and which are used for breeding eels and other species of fish.*

OCA "ROSTA" CON IL SEDANO

Roast duck with celery

1 young duck
    (3-4 kg/7-8 lb)
100 g/3$^{1}/_{2}$ oz bacon fat
1 celery stalk (plus an
    entire head to
    accompany)
Rosemary
Vegetable stock (see p. 34)
White wine
Olive oil

Servings: 8-10	
Preparation time: 20′	
Cooking time: 1h 30′	
Difficulty: ●●	
Flavour: ●●	
Kcal (per serving): 1161	
Proteins (per serving): 37	
Fats (per serving): 103	
Nutritional content: ●●●	

1 Prepare the plucked duck for cooking, removing the innards, the head and neck, the feet and the wingtips. Singe and then wash and dry. Chop up the bacon fat with a few sprigs of rosemary, mix with the chopped celery and a pinch of salt; fill the stomach cavity with this mixture, then sew up the flap and tie up the bird so that it keeps its shape.

2 Put the duck in a an ovenproof dish trickled with oil, rub the skin with salt and set in a pre-heated oven at 170-180 °C. As soon as it begins to brown, pour over $^{1}/_{4}$ litre/8 fl oz/1 cup of wine. When this has evaporated, continue basting with ladlefuls of hot vegetable stock. Cooking will take at least an hour and a half. Serve the duck with strips of raw celery dressed with oil, salt and pepper.

1

2

"PAETA ROSTA COL MALGARAGNO"

Roast turkey with pomegranate

Prepare the plucked turkey-hen for cooking. Remove the innards (keeping the heart and liver to one side) the head and neck, the feet and the wing-tips. Singe, then wash and dry. Season the inside with salt and pepper in moderation, then wrap the breast with strips of bacon fat, securing them with kitchen string or toothpicks. Place in a greased oven-proof dish and set in a pre-heated oven at 180 °C. After a good hour, baste the turkey with the juice of two squeezed pomegranates and with its own cooking juices, and sprinkle with salt. In the meantime, clean and chop the heart and liver; brown them in a frying-pan in 2-3 tablespoons of oil and season with salt and pepper, sprinkling over the juice of the third pomegranate. When the turkey is cooked (after another twenty minutes) remove from the oven, set it on a serving-dish, spoon the sauce over it and carve the servings at table.

1 hen turkey (about 2 kg/ 4 1/2 lb)
100 g/3 1/2 oz bacon fat (thinly sliced)
3 pomegranates
Olive oil

Servings:	6-8
Preparation time:	20'
Cooking time:	1h 30'
Difficulty:	●●
Flavour:	●●
Kcal (per serving):	687
Proteins (per serving):	56
Fats (per serving):	44
Nutritional content:	●●●

91

"PASTIZADA" VENETA

Braised beef

1 Spike the meat with slices of garlic, cloves and cinnamon, set it in a bowl and cover with vinegar and wine in equal proportions. Leave to marinate for 8-10 hours.

2 Peel and chop the onion, and sauté in 60 g/2 oz of melted butter in a casserole. Drain, dry and lightly flour the beef and place in the casserole.

3 Brown slowly, turning so that the meat is evenly-coloured on all sides, then pour over a glass of wine and season with salt and pepper.

4 Cover the casserole with a sheet of lightly-buttered greaseproof paper, then put the lid on top. Cook over a very gentle heat for an hour. Serve the *pastizada* not too hot, cut into slices, with the sauce spooned over.

600 g/1¼ lb rump beef	White wine	Cooking time: 1h 10'
Half an onion	90 g/3 oz butter	Difficulty: ●●
2 cloves garlic		Flavour: ●●
Flour		Kcal (per serving): 412
Cloves		Proteins (per serving): 32
Cinnamon	Servings: 4	Fats (per serving): 21
Vinegar	Prep. time: 20' + 8-10h	Nutritional content: ●●

"POLASTRO IN TECIA"

Pullet with tomato and vegetable sauce

1 chicken (1.2 kg/2³/4 lb)
350 g/12 oz tomato purée
150 g/5 oz cultivated
    mushrooms
1 carrot
1 onion
1 stalk celery
Flour or potato flour
    (to bind the sauce)
Cloves
Powdered cinnamon
Dry white wine
Polenta (to accompany)
50 g/2 oz butter (a little
    may also be needed to
    bind the sauce)
Olive oil

Servings: 4

Preparation time: 25′

Cooking time: 50′

Difficulty: ●●

Flavour: ●●

Kcal (per serving): 1164

Proteins (per serving): 53

Fats (per serving): 65

Nutritional content: ●●●

1 Trim and wash the mushrooms. Prepare the plucked chicken for cooking by removing the innards, head and neck. Singe, wash and dry it, then chop it into pieces and brown them over a rapid heat in a frying-pan in 4-5 tablespoons of oil.
When the pieces are evenly browned, pour over half a glass of wine and let it evaporate.

2 Peel the onion, carrot and celery and chop finely, then sauté in the melted butter and 3-4 tablespoons of oil in a casserole (preferably earthenware).

3 Add the chicken pieces, a pinch of salt, a few cloves, a pinch of powdered cinnamon, the chopped mushrooms and the tomato purée. Stir thoroughly and cook over a medium-high heat for about half an hour.

4 If the sauce should be too liquid, when the chicken is cooked you can thicken it using a little flour or cornflour and a few knobs of butter. Arrange the chicken pieces on a serving-dish, pour over the sauce, and serve with polenta.

PUNTA DI PETTO ALLA TIROLESE

Stuffed breast of veal, Tyrolese style

1 Set the bread crumb to steep in a cup of milk 10 minutes before you start. Peel the onion and chop it finely, then sauté in a frying-pan in the melted butter.

2 Drain the onions and tip them into a bowl with the egg yolks, 6-7 tablespoons of grated Parmesan, the diced ham, a finely-chopped sprig of parsley, the squeezed-out bread, salt, pepper and a pinch of nutmeg and mix well together.

3 When the stuffing is thoroughly blended, spoon it into the pocket of the breast of veal, then sew up the edges with kitchen thread to avoid it leaking out. Set the meat in a casserole with 4-5 tablespoons of oil.

4 Brown the meat over a lively heat; when it is evenly coloured all over, pour over a glass of wine. Lower the heat, cover the casserole and cook gently for another 25 minutes. Serve the breast of veal sliced, accompanied with boiled cabbage, (preferably "black", that is dark-leafed Tuscan cabbage, or kale), dressed with salt, pepper and oil.

500 g/1 lb 2 oz breast of veal (slit open in the form of a pocket)	One slice of white bread (without crust)	Boiled cabbage (to accompany)	Cooking time: 35′
	Parsley	40 g/1¹/₂ oz butter	Difficulty: ●●●
2 onions	Nutmeg	Olive oil	Flavour: ●●
3 egg yolks	Grated Parmesan cheese		Kcal (per serving): 478
50 g/2 oz ham (in one piece)	Milk	Servings: 4	Proteins (per serving): 43
	Dry white wine	Preparation time: 25′ + 10′	Fats (per serving): 19
			Nutritional content: ●●

STRUDEL DI CARNE

Meat strudel

500 g/1 lb 2 oz minced beef (or roast meat leftovers)
300 g/11 oz flour
150 g/5 oz apples
1 whole egg and 1 yolk
Roast beef gravy (or stock cube)
50 g/2 oz pine kernels
Sugar
100 g/3^1/$_2$ oz butter

Servings: 6
Preparation time: 30′ + 30′
Cooking time: 50′ + 5′
Difficulty: ●●●
Flavour: ●●
Kcal (per serving): 501
Proteins (per serving): 26
Fats (per serving): 19
Nutritional content: ●●

1 Heap the flour in the centre of a floured work-surface, adding a tablespoon of sugar and a pinch of salt, then rub in the egg and half the butter cut into flakes. Knead to a soft, pliable dough, roll into a ball, wrap in a moistened tea-cloth and leave to rest for half an hour.

98

2 If you are using minced meat, brown it briefly in a frying-pan in 2-3 tablespoons of oil. If, instead, you have leftovers of roast beef or veal, just chop them in the food processor. Peel the apples and cut into small slices, then tip into a bowl with the meat, the pine kernels, salt, pepper and a few tablespoons of the roast gravy (if you haven't got any, use half a stock cube dissolved in warm water).

3 Roll out the pastry into a thin sheet, and brush it with 20 g/²/₃ oz of melted butter.

4 Spread the stuffing in the centre of the pastry, leaving the edges free, then roll up carefully and seal the ends. Place the meat strudel in a buttered ovenproof dish and brush with the beaten egg yolk. Cook in a pre-heated oven at 180 °C for fifty minutes.

"TONCO DE PONTESÈL"

Meat sauce

1 Peel the onion and chop it up fine, then sauté lightly with the diced bacon fat in a casserole in 2-3 tablespoons of oil. Chop the different meats into evenly-sized chunks and coat lightly in flour, slice the sausage, then tip all into the casserole.

2 Adjust salt and pepper to taste and stir thoroughly, then pour over a glass of wine and let it evaporate over a very low heat.

3 In a small saucepan toast two tablespoons of flour. Add ½ litre/1 pint/2 cups of stock, and gradually blend in over a medium heat. Tip the sauce into the meat casserole, cover, and leave to cook slowly for about an hour and a half, making sure that the sauce doesn't become too thick.

4 Ten minutes before the cooking time is up, remove the cover from the casserole and add a tablespoon of tomato concentrate diluted in a little hot water. Serve the delicious sauce surrounded by a golden crown of polenta.

250 g/9 oz lean pork	1 onion	(to accompany, see p. 68)	**Cooking time:** 1h 45'
250 g/9 oz veal	Flour		**Difficulty:** ●●
150 g/5 oz beef	Tomato concentrate	Olive oil	**Flavour:** ●●
1 fresh lucanica (or other fresh pork sausage)	Vegetable stock (see p. 34)		**Kcal (per serving):** 740
			Proteins (per serving): 33
50 g/2 oz bacon fat (in one slice)	Dry white wine	**Servings:** 6	**Fats (per serving):** 30
	Polenta	**Preparation time:** 30'	**Nutritional content:** ●●

The name lucanica *(better known as* luganega *or* luganiga) *derives from* Lucania, *whence the ancient Romans imported it to north-eastern Italy. Normally eaten fresh, it is a long, thin sausage made of pure pork, both fat and lean with salt and spices packed into gut lining. However, any other fresh sausage can be used, or even minced pork. The origins of the curious name of this substantial dish remain a mystery; there are those who claim that it is connected with the fact that, in the days before the refrigerator, people would keep perishable foodstuffs and leftovers on the* pontesèl *outside the house.*

STUFATO DI CASTRATO

Mutton stew

7-800 g/1^1/$_2$ lb shoulder
  or leg of mutton
  (boned)
1 carrot
2 onions
1 stalk celery
1 clove garlic
Parsley
Sage
Dry white wine
Olive oil

Servings:	4
Preparation time:	20'
Cooking time:	about 2h
Difficulty:	●●
Flavour:	●●
Kcal (per serving):	316
Proteins (per serving):	35
Fats (per serving):	11
Nutritional content:	●

1 Peel the onions, carrot and celery and chop them roughly. Tip them into a casserole with a few leaves of sage, a finely-chopped sprig of parsley and the squashed garlic clove. Set the mutton on top, pour over a trickle of oil, then cover the meat with water, adding a generous pinch of salt. Put the lid on the casserole and turn on the heat.

2 Simmer slowly until all the water has evaporated, then remove the lid and let the meat brown nicely in the sauce. After 6-7 minutes pour over half a glass of wine and let it evaporate. Keeping the heat low, let the sauce reduce for a further 10 minutes, then serve the stew piping hot with the accompaniment of your choice.

"POENTA E OSEI" ALLA VICENTINA

Polenta with birds, Vicenza style

6-8 small birds (warblers, ortolans or thrushes)
100 g/3¹/₂ oz bacon fat
Sage
Polenta (see p. 68)
60 g/2 oz butter

Servings:	4
Preparation time:	20'
Cooking time:	about 2h
Difficulty:	●●
Flavour:	●●
Kcal (per serving):	721
Proteins (per serving):	27
Fats (per serving):	43
Nutritional content:	●●

Pluck, singe, wash and dry the birds, removing the feet. Traditionally they should be cooked with their innards, but if the idea does not appeal, remove them and put a little salt and pepper and a sage leaf into the stomach cavity. Again traditionally, the birds should be cooked on the spit, alternating them with slices of bacon fat sandwiched between leaves of sage. If you don't have access to a spit or an open fire, then wrap the birds in bacon and sage and set them in an ovenproof dish, dotting with flakes of butter. Cook them in a pre-heated oven at 180 °C for twenty minutes. Sprinkle with salt, baste the birds with their cooking juices, then replace in the oven for about another twenty minutes. In the meantime prepare a not too stiff polenta, turn it out onto a board in the centre of the table, and lay the birds on top, spooning over the exquisite sauce.

TRIPPA ALLA TREVISANA ▸

Tripe, Treviso style

1 kg/2¹/₄ lb calves' tripe	Slices of toasted bread	**Servings:** 6		**Kcal (per serving):** 823	
100 g/3¹/₂ oz bacon fat	(to accompany)	**Preparation time:** 20′		**Proteins (per serving):** 36	
1 onion	Stock (preferably beef)	**Cooking time:** 40′		**Fats (per serving):** 57	
Rosemary	50 g/2 oz butter	**Difficulty:** ●●		**Nutritional content:** ●●●	
Grated Parmesan cheese		**Flavour:** ●●			

1 Peel the onion, chop it up small and sauté gently in the melted butter in a casserole with the diced bacon fat and the leaves of a sprig of rosemary. Wash the tripe, cut it into thin strips and tip into the casserole.

2 Let the tripe colour lightly, stirring all the time, then pour over a few ladlefuls of stock, seasoning with salt and pepper. Leave to simmer gently for half an hour, so that the liquid reduces gradually. Serve the tripe, sprinkled generously with Parmesan, with slices of toasted bread.

"POENTA E OSELETI SCAPAI"

Polenta with skewered meats

6 slices of hard polenta (see p. 68)
400 g/14 oz loin of veal
120 g/4 oz bacon fat (in one slice)
150 g/5 oz cultivated mushrooms
6 chicken livers
Sage
100g/3¹/₂ oz butter

Servings: 6	
Preparation time: 20′	
Cooking time: 40′	
Difficulty: ●●	
Flavour: ●●	
Kcal (per serving): 563	
Proteins (per serving): 23	
Fats (per serving): 37	
Nutritional content: ●●	

Trim and wash the mushrooms, then slice them. Clean the chicken livers, slice and sauté in a frying-pan with 30 g/1 oz butter. Chop the veal into chunks, and make up one skewer for each person, alternating the chunks of veal with the diced bacon fat, the slices of liver and the mushrooms, all separated by leaves of sage. Lay the skewers in an ovenproof dish, season with salt and pepper and dot with the remaining butter in flakes. Cook in a pre-heated oven at 180 °C for about half an hour. Meanwhile fry the slices of polenta and arrange on a serving-dish. Remove the skewers from the oven, lay on top of the polenta, and serve.

"TORRESANI DE BREGANZE"

Breganze pigeons

4 pigeons
80 g/3 oz bacon fat
    (thinly sliced)
2 cloves garlic
Rosemary, sage
Juniper berries
Cinnamon, cloves, nutmeg
Olive oil

Servings: 4	
Preparation time: 20'	
Cooking time: 55'	
Difficulty: ●●	
Flavour: ●●	
Kcal (per serving): 629	
Proteins (per serving): 38	
Fats (per serving): 51	
Nutritional content: ●●	

Finely chop the garlic with the leaves from a sprig of rosemary, a few sage leaves, a teaspoon of juniper berries, a piece of cinnamon and 3-4 cloves, then add a pinch of grated nutmeg. Prepare the plucked pigeons: remove the innards, singe, wash and dry them, sprinkle salt and pepper in the stomach cavity, then wrap them up in strips of bacon fat. If they are to be cooked on the spit, take care to brush them with oil, and when half-cooked (after about 40 minutes, sprinkle them with the chopped herb and spice mixture, and cook for a further 40 minutes. Otherwise, they can be cooked in the oven. In this case insert a little of the herb and spice mixture into the stomach cavity, they lay in an ovenproof dish and cook in a pre-heated oven at 180 °C. After half an hour, remove and baste with the cooking juices, sprinkle with the remaining herb and spice mixture and replace in the oven for another 20-25 minutes. Serve with fried polenta and green salad.

This manner of preparing pigeons - known as torresani *in Veneto and as* torraioli *in other parts of Italy, although the former is a noun and the latter an adjective – is characteristic of the area of Breganze, in the region of Vicenza.*

FISH
AND MOLLUSCS

6

BACCALÀ ALLA CAPPUCCINA

Salt cod with raisins and pine kernels

---

1 kg/2¹/4 lb salt cod
    (already steeped)
2 cloves garlic
Parsley
Milk
Pine kernels and raisins
50 g/2 oz butter
Olive oil

Servings: 6	
Preparation time: 20′	
Cooking time: 30′	
Difficulty: ●●	
Flavour: ●●	
Kcal (per serving): 527	
Proteins (per serving): 45	
Fats (per serving): 29	
Nutritional content: ●●	

1 Cut the salt cod into fairly large pieces, set them in a casserole and cover with cold water. Turn on the heat and, as soon as the water comes to the boil, take out the pieces of cod, drain and remove the skin, bones and any hard pieces. Sauté the cloves of garlic lightly in a frying-pan in the melted butter and 2-3 tablespoons of oil, removing them as soon as they begin to colour.

2 Put the cod in the frying-pan, and season with a pinch of pepper (salt is probably not required) and a finely-chopped sprig of parsley. Cook over a very gentle heat, pouring over a ladleful of warm milk from time to time as it is gradually absorbed, and stirring delicately. After about ten minutes you should have a nice thick sauce and the cod should be nearly cooked. Tip in a tablespoon of raisins and one of pine-kernels, and leave the flavours to blend for another 4-5 minutes.

In Veneto, Friuli and Trentino cod preserved in salt is usually called baccalà *while the fish dried traditionally in the wind and sun is called* stoccafisso *(stockfish). Although this rule does not always hold, all the recipes here can be successfully prepared with both types.*

Baccalà Mantecato

Cream of salt cod

Cut the salt cod into pieces, set them in a casserole and cover with cold water. Turn on the heat and, as soon as the water comes to the boil, remove the pieces of cod with a fish slice and drain. Remove the skin, bones and any hard pieces, then put them in an earthenware casserole rubbed with garlic, and season very moderately with salt. Over a very gentle heat, break up the cod with a wooden spoon; stirring all the time, very gradually add a glass of warm milk and one of olive oil, mixing in spoonfuls of each alternately. Finally, after about twenty minutes, the fish should have been reduced to a soft but firm cream. This sophisticated Venetian speciality, related to the *brandade niçoise,* is now ready to be served.

1 kg/2 1/4 lb salt cod
    (already steeped)
Milk
1 clove garlic
Olive oil

Servings: 6
Preparation time: 5′
Cooking time: 30′
Difficulty: ●●
Flavour: ●●
Kcal (per serving): 347
Protein (per serving): 39
Fats (per serving): 18
Nutritional content: ●

Baccalà alla Vicentina

Salt cod, Vicenza style

1 Trim the salt cod, removing bones and any hard pieces but leaving the skin on, then cut into pieces. Coat lightly in flour and arrange in an oven-proof dish without overlapping. Sprinkle with salt, pepper, a pinch of powdered cinnamon and plenty of grated Parmesan.

2 Peel the onion and chop it up fine with the garlic, then sauté in a frying-pan in 6-7 tablespoons of oil.

3 Trim, wash and fillet the anchovies, and blend them into the onion mixture with the help of a wooden spoon. Add a finely-chopped sprig of parsley and pour over a glass of wine.

The historic chess game, the Gioco degli Scacchi, *in the piazza of Marostica (Vicenza).*

1 kg/2¹/4 lb salt cod (already steeped)	³/4 litre/1¹/2 pt/3 cups milk	40 g/1¹/2 oz butter Olive oil	**Cooking time:** 2h 10′
			Difficulty: ●●●
Flour	Powdered cinnamon		**Flavour:** ●●
4 anchovies	Grated Parmesan cheese		**Kcal (per serving):** 777
1 onion	Dry white wine		**Proteins (per serving):** 54
1 clove garlic	Polenta (see p. 68, to	**Servings:** 6	**Fats (per serving):** 26
Parsley	accompany)	**Preparation time:** 15′	**Nutritional content:** ●●

4 Once the wine has evaporated, pour over the milk and blend the butter into the sauce. Pour the sauce over the cod in the ovenproof dish, cover and set in a pre-heated oven at 160 °C. Cooking is complete when the liquid has been completely absorbed, and should continue for as long as possible, at least two hours. If you have time, set the oven to 140 °C instead and cook the cod for another hour. Serve this delicious dish with slices of firm polenta.

"BISATO IN TECIA"

Fried eels in tomato sauce

		Servings: 6	Fats (per serving): 69
1.5 kg/3^1/$_2$ lb medium-size eels	Dry Marsala	Preparation time: 30′ + 4-5h	Nutritional content: ●●●
500 g/1 lb 2 oz tomato purée	Polenta (see p. 68, to accompany)	Cooking time: 25′	
2 cloves garlic	40 g/1^1/$_2$ oz butter	Difficulty: ●●	
Bay leaves, parsley, sage	Vinegar	Flavour: ●●●	
Breadcrumbs	Olive oil	Kcal (per serving): 1233	
		Proteins (per serving): 47	

1 Clean and skin the eels (although this is not necessary if they are small) and remove the heads. Cut them into pieces about 6-7 cm/2 ^{1}/$_2$ in long, rinse under cold running water and dry. Set them in a bowl with 5-6 tablespoons of oil, a glass of vinegar, 2 or 3 bay leaves, a few sage leaves, salt and pepper, and leave to marinate for 4-5 hours.

2 Sauté the squashed garlic cloves lightly in a frying-pan in the melted butter and a couple of spoonfuls of oil. Remove the eel chunks from the marinade, drain, dry and coat lightly in breadcrumbs, then place in the frying-pan.

3 Fry the breaded eel pieces rapidly over a lively heat, turning frequently so that they become evenly coloured all over, then pour over half a glass of Marsala.

4 When the Marsala has evaporated, pour in the tomato purée and season with salt and pepper. Leave to cook over a medium heat, letting the sauce reduce, for a good quarter of an hour. When cooked, sprinkle with chopped parsley and serve the eels with sliced polenta.

113

"BISATI" AL LIMONE

Eels in lemon

1 kg/2^{1}/4 lb small eels
3 lemons
Bay leaves

Servings: 4	
Preparation time: 20'	
Cooking time: 15'	
Difficulty: ●●	
Flavour: ●●	
Kcal (per serving): 628	
Proteins (per serving): 38	
Fats (per serving): 50	
Nutritional content: ●●	

As of course you know, small eels don't need to be skinned. Clean them, cut the heads off and chop into lengths of about 6-7 cm/2 ^{1}/2 in. Rinse, dry and line them up in a fireproof dish (preferably earthenware) slipping bay leaves in between them. Season with salt and pepper, then sprinkle with the juice of the lemons. Cook over a lively heat for a quarter of an hour, letting the juices reduce, then serve the eels piping hot.
As you will see no fat of either vegetable or animal derivation is used in this delicious and fragrant dish, which can also be served in small portions as an antipasto.

L "BOSEGA" IN SALSA AROMATICA

Mullet in aromatic sauce

1 Clean the mullet, removing the innards, then wash it and place in a casserole. Cover with cold water, adding a pinch of salt, a tablespoon of vinegar and a few sprigs of parsley. Put the lid on the casserole, bring to the boil and simmer gently. After about half an hour remove the fish, drain, and set on a serving-dish, garnished with sage. Meanwhile boil the egg for 7 minutes.

2 Steep the bread crumb in vinegar, then squeeze it out and whiz in the food processor with the washed and filleted anchovies, the yolk of the hard-boiled egg, a tablespoon of capers, 5-6 stoned olives, a sprig of parsley and a pinch of pepper. Tip into a bowl and, stirring all the time, gradually dribble in enough oil to produce a fairly thick sauce; complete by stirring in the lemon juice.

1 mullet (about 1 kg/ 2¹/₄ lb)
2 slices of white bread (without crust)
2 anchovies
1 lemon
1 egg
Capers
Sage
Pickled olives
Parsley
Vinegar
Olive oil

Servings:	4
Preparation time:	25'
Cooking time:	37'
Difficulty:	●●
Flavour:	●●
Kcal (per serving):	593
Proteins (per serving):	47
Fats (per serving):	33
Nutritional content:	●●

PERSICO ALLA TRIESTINA

Perch, Trieste style

600 g/1 1/4 lb perch fillets
400 g/14 oz cockles or
    clams
1 clove garlic
2 eggs
Parsley
Breadcrumbs
Fried celery (to accompany)
Olive oil
Oil for frying

Servings: 4	
Preparation time: 20'	
Cooking time: 25'	
Difficulty: ●●	
Flavour: ●●	
Kcal (per serving): 499	
Proteins (per serving): 30	
Fats (per serving): 38	
Nutritional content: ●●	

1 Skin the perch fillets and flatten them out slightly. Rinse the shell-fish, then tip them into a frying-pan with a trickle of oil and let them open over a lively heat.

2 Remove the shells and replace the molluscs in the frying-pan with the squashed garlic clove and a pinch of pepper. Sauté for two minutes, again over a lively heat.

3 Season the perch lightly with salt and pepper and spread the molluscs over them with a little finely-chopped parsley, then double the fillets over lengthwise.

4 Dip first into the beaten egg and then into the breadcrumbs, repeating the operation twice, then fry in plenty of boiling oil. Remove as soon as the fish is golden, and drain on kitchen paper. Serve with generous portions of fried celery.

POLPI E FAGIOLI IN CORONA

Baby octopus and beans with polenta

1 Steep the beans for at least 5-6 hours in advance. Drain, tip into a large saucepan and cover with lightly salted water (not too much, since when cooked the beans should be almost dry). Put the lid on the saucepan, set over a very gentle heat and simmer for three-quarters of an hour.

2 Clean the octopus, wash under running water, and chop into pieces. Clean, wash and fillet the anchovy, then mash it up in 3-4 tablespoons of oil in a casserole, and pour over half a glass of wine. Add a tablespoon of tomato concentrate, salt and pepper, and mix well, then tip in the octopus pieces. Pour over a ladleful of hot water, cover the casserole and leave to simmer for about an hour.

3 When the liquid is almost completely absorbed, add the drained beans, adjust salt and pepper to taste, stir well and leave the flavours to blend for about ten minutes.

4 Prepare the polenta, following the instructions on page 68, making sure it is fairly stiff. Transfer it to a ring mould (with a fairly broad hole) level off the surface and keep warm in the oven or in a bain-marie. Turn the polenta out onto a round serving-dish, fill the central hole with the octopus and bean mixture, and serve.

		Servings: 6	Fats (per serving): 23
500 g/1 lb 2 oz Lamon or borlotti beans	Tomato concentrate Red wine	Preparation time: 30' + 5-6h	Nutritional content: ●●
1 kg/2¼ lb small octopus	30 g/1 oz butter Olive oil	Cooking time: 2h 40'	
200 g/7 oz cornmeal (for polenta, see p. 68)		Difficulty: ●●	
1 anchovy		Flavour: ●●●	
		Kcal (per serving): 669	
		Proteins (per serving): 36	

200 g/7 oz cornmeal (for polenta, see p. 68)

ROMBO AL RADICCHIO

Turbot with red chicory

6-700 g/1¹/₄-1¹/₂ lb
  turbot fillets
1 head Treviso (long-leafed)
  red chicory
1 onion
1 clove garlic
4 anchovy fillets in oil
Bay leaves (also to garnish)
Boiled potatoes (to
  accompany)
Olive oil

Servings: 4	
Preparation time: 5′	
Cooking time: 20′	
Difficulty: ●●	
Flavour: ●●	
Kcal (per serving): 425	
Proteins (per serving): 38	
Fats (per serving): 15	
Nutritional content: ●●	

1 Peel the onion and cut it into thin slices or rings. Wash and trim the chicory, then set it on a chopping-board and slice it finely crosswise.

2 Sauté the onion, the chicory and the drained anchovy fillets gently in a frying-pan in 4-5 tablespoons of oil, seasoning with salt and pepper to taste.

3 In another frying-pan sauté gently the finely-chopped garlic and a crumbled bay leaf in 3-4 tablespoons of oil. Tip in the turbot fillets cut into evenly-sized strips, and sauté for about 4 minutes.

4 Season with salt and pepper, then tip the fish into the frying-pan with the onion and chicory. Mix well, let the flavours blend for about 5 minutes, then serve immediately accompanied with boiled potatoes.

SARDONI "ALA CIOSOTA"

Pilchards, Chioggia style

1 kg/2¹/4 lb large pilchards
1 carrot
1 onion
2 stalks celery
1 clove garlic
Parsley
Polenta (see p. 68, to
    accompany)
Dry white wine
Olive oil

Servings: 6	
Preparation time: 20'	
Cooking time: 10'	
Difficulty: ●●	
Flavour: ●●●	
Kcal (per serving): 590	
Proteins (per serving): 30	
Fats (per serving): 20	
Nutritional content: ●●	

Clean the pilchards, remove the heads and wash under cold running water.

Peel the onion, trim and scrape the carrot and celery, then chop them roughly and sauté with the garlic in a large frying-pan in 5-6 tablespoons of oil. Dry the pilchards and set them in the frying-pan, then pour over a glass of wine, sprinkle with chopped parsley and season with salt and pepper. Cook over a gentle heat for 7-8 minutes, then serve the pilchards *ala ciosota* (or Chioggia style) piping hot with polenta.

SARDONI ALLA GRECA

Pilchards, Greek style

1 kg/2¹/4 lb large pilchards
1 clove garlic
Parsley
Vinegar
Olive oil

Servings: 6	
Preparation time: 20'	
Cooking time: 25'	
Difficulty: ●●	
Flavour: ●●●	
Kcal (per serving): 329	
Proteins (per serving): 26	
Fats (per serving): 23	
Nutritional content: ●	

Clean the pilchards, remove the heads and wash under cold running water. Set them in an ovenproof dish with 5-6 tablespoons of oil, the garlic and a sprig of parsley, both chopped, a pinch of salt and half a glass of vinegar (if you wish, you can substitute this with lemon juice). Set the dish in a pre-heated oven at 180 °C for about 25 minutes and serve piping hot (although they are also delicious cold).

"SEPIE ALA CIOSOTA"

Cuttlefish, Chioggia style

800 g/1¾ lb medium-size cuttlefish
2 anchovies
1 onion
1 clove garlic
Half a lemon
Parsley
Polenta (see p. 68, to accompany)
Dry white wine
Olive oil

Servings:	4
Preparation time:	20'
Cooking time:	40'
Difficulty:	●●
Flavour:	●●●
Kcal (per serving):	502
Proteins (per serving):	26
Fats (per serving):	17
Nutritional content:	●●

Clean the cuttlefish (removing the cuttlebone, the ink sacs and the eyes), wash them and cut into strips, chopping the tentacles up small. Wash the anchovies under running water, then fillet them. Peel the onion and slice thinly, then put it into a casserole with the cuttlefish, the garlic chopped fine with a sprig of parsley and 7-8 tablespoons of oil. Sauté briefly, stirring all the time, then pour over a glass of wine and add the roughly-chopped anchovies (because of the anchovies, salt is hardly necessary). Cook slowly for about half an hour, stirring all the time. Turn off the heat, sprinkle with lemon juice and serve the cuttlefish nice and hot with little piles of polenta (see instructions on page 68). This dish provides a succulent complete meal, to be rounded off with a fruit tart.

"SEPIE ALA VENEXIANA"

Cuttlefish, Venetian style

Clean the cuttlefish (removing the cuttlebone and the eyes), wash them and cut into strips, chopping the tentacles up small. Don't forget to keep a couple of ink sacs to one side.

Sauté the clove of garlic in a casserole in 4-5 tablespoons of oil, and remove it as soon as it begins to colour.

Tip in the cuttlefish, a pinch of salt and pepper, and cook very gently for half an hour letting the molluscs cook slowly in the water they release. After this, pour over half a glass of wine and add the ink sacs, then let the sauce reduce gradually, stirring all the time. Serve the cuttlefish hot over little heaps of polenta, sprinkled with chopped parsley.

800 g/1 3/4 lb medium-size cuttlefish
1 clove garlic
Parsley
Polenta (see p. 68, to accompany)
Dry white wine
Olive oil

Servings:	4
Preparation time:	20'
Cooking time:	35'
Difficulty:	●●
Flavour:	●●●
Kcal (per serving):	475
Proteins (per serving):	26
Fats (per serving):	14
Nutritional content:	●●

"SEPIE IN TECIA COI BISI"

Cuttlefish with tomato and peas

800 g/1³/4 lb medium-size
   cuttlefish
300 g/11 oz shelled peas
1 onion
1 celery heart
1 clove garlic
100 g/3¹/2 oz peeled
   tomatoes
Parsley
Polenta (see p. 68,
   to accompany)
Dry white wine
Olive oil

Servings: 4	
Preparation time: 30'	
Cooking time: 40'	
Difficulty: ●●	
Flavour: ●●●	
Kcal (per serving): 578	
Proteins (per serving): 39	
Fats (per serving): 15	
Nutritional content: ●●	

1 Clean the cuttlefish (removing the cuttlebone, the ink sacs and the eyes), wash them and cut into strips, chopping the tentacles up small. Peel the onion and trim the celery, then chop finely and sauté in a casserole in 5-6 tablespoons of oil, with salt and pepper and the whole clove of garlic. Remove the garlic and add the cuttlefish, then blend thoroughly over a lively heat and pour over half a glass of wine.

2 Let the wine evaporate, then add the peas, the peeled tomatoes and a ladelful of hot water. Cover the casserole and cook slowly over a gentle heat for half an hour. Just before the time is up, remove the lid, add a finely-chopped sprig of parsley and let the sauce reduce. Serve the cuttlefish in their sauce with steaming polenta.

900 g/2 lb sole (4 medium or 8 small fish)
1 egg
1 lemon (plus another to garnish)
1 shallot
Flour
Parsley
Olive oil
Oil for frying

Servings:	4
Preparation time:	25' + 1h
Cooking time:	20'
Difficulty:	●●
Flavour:	●●●
Kcal (per serving):	586
Proteins (per serving):	39
Fats (per serving):	42
Nutritional content:	●●

SOGLIOLE ALLA TRIESTINA

Sole, Trieste style

1 Clean the sole, skin and wash them. Dry them and lay in a bowl with 5-6 tablespoons of oil, lemon juice, the chopped shallot and parsley, salt and pepper and leave to marinate for an hour.

2 Drain the sole of its marinade, and dip into a batter made with the beaten egg and a tablespoon of flour. Fry in plenty of boiling oil, then lay to dry on kitchen paper, and salt lightly. Serve immediately, garnished with slices of lemon.

"Sfogi in saór"

Pickled sole

1 Clean and fillet the sole, then wash and dry the fillets, season with salt and pepper and coat lightly in flour. Fry in a frying-pan in 7-8 tablespoons of oil over a moderate heat for 5-6 minutes each side; drain and lay in a dish.

2 Peel and trim the onion and celery and scrape the carrot, then chop them roughly. Sauté gently for a good quarter of an hour in the pan where you have fried the sole, adding another 7-8 tablespoons of oil and a ladleful of stock, with a pinch of salt and two bay leaves.

3 Tip the sautéed vegetables with their juices into the dish with the sole, spread the mixture evenly, then sprinkle over the raisins and pine kernels.

4 Pour a glass of vinegar and one of wine into the frying-pan and reduce rapidly over a lively heat, then pour this over the contents of the dish. Keep in a cool place for a couple of hours before serving.

		Servings: 4	Fats (per serving): 19
4 sole (900 g/2 lb)	Flour	Preparation time: 30' + 3h	Nutritional content: ●●
2 carrots	Vegetable stock (see p. 34)	Cooking time: 30'	
1 onion	Vinegar	Difficulty: ●●	
1 celery heart	Dry white wine	Flavour: ●●●	
Bay leaves	Olive oil	Kcal (per serving): 472	
30 g/1 oz pine kernels		Proteins (per serving): 40	
30 g/1 oz raisins			

This exquisite cold dish – which can also be served in small portions as an antipasto – was traditionally eaten by the Venetians on the Feast of the Redeemer (third Sunday in July).

SOGLIOLE IN CREMA DI GAMBERI

Sole with shrimp sauce

1 Clean and fillet the sole, then wash and dry the fillets. Prepare the *fumet* by dissolving the fish stock cube in half a litre/1 pint of boiling water. Scald the shrimps in lightly salted water, drain and remove the heads and shells (which you should keep aside and whiz in the food processor). Place the peeled shrimps in a bowl and cover with a little of the hot *fumet* .

2 Cream 80 g/3 oz of butter in a bowl with a wooden spoon, then blend in the shrimp-shell purée, adding a pinch of salt and pepper.

A view of the Grand Canal in Venice.

3

4

2 sole (800 g/1³/₄ lb)
300 g/11 oz shrimps
Fish *fumet* (stock cube)
Flour
120 g/4 oz butter

Servings: 4	
Preparation time: 30' + 3 h	
Cooking time: 30'	
Difficulty: ●●	
Flavour: ●●	
Kcal (per serving): 513	
Proteins (per serving): 45	
Fats (per serving): 31	
Nutritional content: ●●	

3 Coat the sole fillets lightly in flour, line them up in a well-buttered ovenproof dish and cover with the fish *fumet*. Cover with a sheet of aluminium foil, then put the lid on the dish and set in a pre-heated oven at 180 °C for 15 minutes. Remove the fillets and set them on a hot serving-dish, keeping the cooking juices to one side.

4 Tip the sole cooking juices into a saucepan with the shrimps and the creamed butter. Warm over a gentle heat, stirring all the time. Season with salt and pepper, adding a few spoonfuls of *fumet* if the sauce should seem too thick. Serve the sole fillets with the shrimp sauce spooned over: delicious.

131

PESCETTI MARINATI

Marinated fish

		Servings: 6	Fats (per serving): 50
1 kg/2¹/₄ lb small fish	Whole black peppercorns	**Preparation time: 30' + 24h**	Nutritional content: ●●●
Half an onion	Vinegar	**Cooking time: 40'**	
1 carrot	Dry white wine	**Difficulty: ●●**	
1 clove garlic	Olive oil	**Flavour: ●●●**	
Bay leaves, marjoram, sage, basil, parsley	Oil for frying	**Kcal (per serving): 651**	
Flour		**Proteins (per serving): 22**	

Wash and dry the fish, coat them in flour and fry a few at a time in a frying-pan in plenty of boiling oil. Drain well and set them in a dish. Peel the onion and scrape the carrot, then chop them up fine with the garlic; tip into a saucepan with half a litre/1 pint of vinegar, a glass of wine, sprigs of basil, parsley, marjoram and sage, a bay leaf, a few peppercorns, a pinch of salt and half a glass of oil. Boil for about a quarter of an hour, then pour the boiling marinade over the fish. Cover the dish and leave to marinate for at least twenty-four hours. Delicious served with fried polenta as a main course, the fish is also excellent as an antipasto, accompanied by a glass of white wine.

A view of the valli *or fish-ponds, enclosed sections of the lagoon rich in fauna.*

Stoccafisso alla Barcaiola

Stockfish, fisherman style

1 kg/2¹/4 lb stockfish
    (already steeped)
8 anchovies
1 onion
1 clove garlic
1 bay leaf
Parsley
Vinegar
Dry white wine
Olive oil

Servings: 6	
Preparation time: 30'	
Cooking time: 30'	
Difficulty: ●●	
Flavour: ●●●	
Kcal (per serving): 392	
Proteins (per serving): 45	
Fats (per serving): 16	
Nutritional content: ●	

1 Clean, wash and fillet the anchovies and set to one side. Wash the stockfish (stoccafisso, also known as baccalà in many parts of the Triveneto region), set it in a casserole with the garlic and a bay leaf and cover with cold water. Bring to the boil and after five minutes turn off the heat, leaving the fish in the water.

2 Peel the onion and slice finely, then sauté in a frying-pan in 5-6 tablespoons of oil.

3 Pour over two scant glasses of vinegar and one of wine. Add the anchovies and leave to cook for ten minutes then stir in the finely-chopped garlic.

4 Drain the stockfish and set it in an ovenproof dish, then pour over the hot sauce. Mix well, season with salt and pepper and set in a preheated oven at 150-160 °C for 10 minutes.

Different types of fish and shellfish on the stalls of a fish market.

TRIGLIE ALL'ORIENTALE

Red mullet, Eastern style

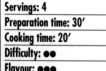

1 kg/2¼ lb red mullet
1 onion
2 tomatoes
Pine kernels
Parsley
Boiled rice (optional, to
    accompany)
Dry white wine
Olive oil

Servings:	4
Preparation time:	30'
Cooking time:	20'
Difficulty:	●●
Flavour:	●●●
Kcal (per serving):	660
Proteins (per serving):	40
Fats (per serving):	24
Nutritional content:	●●

Clean the mullet, removing the innards, and wash and dry them. Peel the onion, chop it up fine and sauté in a frying-pan in 5-6 tablespoons of oil. Add a tablespoon of pine kernels and the mullet, then pour over a glass of wine. Wash and roughly chop the tomatoes and add to the fish, along with a little hot water if necessary. Cook briefly, turning the mullet over very carefully so that they do not break, for 5-6 minutes on each side. Just before cooking is complete, add a chopped sprig of parsley and a pinch of salt. Serve this delicate dish, with its echoes of the Aegean dominion of the *Serenissima*, with plain, boiled rice.

TROTE ALLA TRENTINA

Trout, Trentino style

1 Set a handful of sultanas to steep in warm water half an hour before starting. Clean the trout, then wash and dry them. Coat lightly in flour and fry in a frying-pan in plenty of boiling oil. Drain, salt lightly and lay in a dish.

2 Peel and chop the onion and sauté in a casserole in 2-3 tablespoons of oil. Add half a litre/1 pint of vinegar, the garlic chopped finely with a sprig of parsley, a sprig of mint, the squeezed sultanas and a little grated lemon peel. Bring to the boil, and after 4-5 minutes remove the casserole from the heat. Pour the boiling marinade over the trout and leave to rest in a cool place for 24 hours. Drain the trout, and serve with polenta.

1 kg/2¼ lb rainbow trout
1 onion
2 cloves garlic
1 lemon
Flour
Mint, parsley
Sultanas
Vinegar
Olive oil
Oil for frying

Servings: 4	
Prep. time: 30' + 24h 30'	
Cooking time: 30'	
Difficulty: ●●	
Flavour: ●●●	
Kcal (per serving): 764	
Proteins (per serving): 48	
Fats (per serving): 50	
Nutritional content: ●●●	

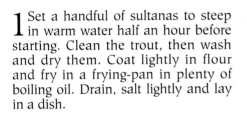

TROTE CON LE MANDORLE

Trout with almonds

1 kg/2¹/₄ lb rainbow trout
100 g/3¹/₂ oz shelled almonds
Raisins
70 g/2¹/₂ oz butter
Servings: 4
Preparation time: 30′ + 40′
Cooking time: 30′
Difficulty: ●●
Flavour: ●●●
Kcal (per serving): 706
Proteins (per serving): 53
Fats (per serving): 44
Nutritional content: ●●●

1 Set a handful of raisins to steep in warm water half an hour before starting, and grind the almonds (or whiz in the food processor). Clean, wash and dry the trout, then sprinkle with salt and leave to rest in a dish for 10 minutes. After this brown them lightly in a frying-pan in 40 g/1¹/₂ oz of butter for 15 minutes, turning them over gently.

2 Remove the fish from the frying-pan and keep warm; sauté the almonds briefly in the pan juices diluted with a knob of butter, then replace the trout along with the squeezed raisins. Let the flavours blend for 4-5 minutes, then serve hot. Again, this delicately-balanced dish recalls Venice's historic trade with the Orient.

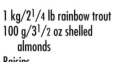

SALADS, RED CHICORY AND CARPACCI

7

CARPACCIO DI MANZO ▸

Beef carpaccio

350 g/12 oz sirloin or fillet
    of beef, very thinly sliced
2 peppers
200 g/7 oz black grapes
1 clove garlic
2 lemons
Sugar
Grana (or Parmesan) cheese
Olive oil

Servings: 4	
Preparation time: 15'	
Cooking time: 10'	
Difficulty: ●	
Flavour: ●	
Kcal (per serving): 466	
Proteins (per serving): 25	
Fats (per serving): 15	
Nutritional content: ●●	

1 Trim the peppers, wash and cut into thin strips. Sauté gently for 10 minutes with the garlic in 5-6 tablespoons of oil in a frying-pan.

2 Drain the peppers and put to one side. Wash and seed the grapes, then cut into slivers and sauté for one minute in the pepper oil.

3 Tip the grapes into a bowl with the peppers, half a glass of fresh olive oil, the lemon juice, salt, pepper and a pinch of sugar; mix well and leave to rest for half an hour. Arrange the slices of beef on a serving-dish, spread them with the marinade, and sprinkle generously with flakes of grana or Parmesan cheese.

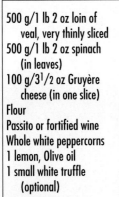

500 g/1 lb 2 oz loin of
    veal, very thinly sliced
500 g/1 lb 2 oz spinach
    (in leaves)
100 g/3^1/2 oz Gruyère
    cheese (in one slice)
Flour
Passito or fortified wine
Whole white peppercorns
1 lemon, Olive oil
1 small white truffle
    (optional)

Servings: 6	
Preparation time: 15' + 45'	
Difficulty: ●	
Flavour: ●	
Kcal (per serving): 516	
Protein (per serving): 51	
Fats (per serving): 19	
Nutritional content: ●●	

CARPACCIO DI VITELLO

Veal carpaccio

Trim the spinach well, wash thoroughly and dry, then chop into very thin strips. Roll out the slices of veal until they are paper-thin, then cut into strips. Lay them on a flat serving-platter, and garnish with a trickle of top quality olive oil, lemon juice, salt, whole white peppercorns and half a glass of passito. Lay the strips of spinach over it, and put in the fridge for three-quarters of an hour. Serve the carpaccio sprinkled with flakes of Gruyère cheese and, if you wish, tiny slivers of fragrant white truffle.

CARPACCIO DI CAPESANTE

Scallop carpaccio

16 scallops (or coquilles St. Jacques)
1 onion
1 carrot
1 yellow pepper
1 zucchino (or courgette)
1 bunch rocket
2 lemons
Olive oil

Servings: 4	
Preparation time: 35' + 1h	
Difficulty: ●	
Flavour: ●●	
Kcal (per serving): 194	
Proteins (per serving): 12	
Fats (per serving): 11	
Nutritional content: ●	

Peel, trim and wash the vegetables, then slice the onion carrot and zucchino thinly. Remove the seeds and the white inner parts from the pepper and dice up small. Tip all the vegetables into a bowl, and dress with the lemon juice, fresh olive oil and salt and pepper to taste. Leave the marinade to rest while you prepare the shellfish. Wash the scallops under cold running water. Open them and remove the white muscle and the coral tongue, cut into thin strips and arrange on a flat serving-dish. Cover with the vegetable marinade and leave to rest for an hour before serving. Trim, wash and dry the rocket and chop it roughly. Arrange on the dish with the scallops and garnish with slices of lemon.

CARPACCIO DI PESCE SPADA

Swordfish carpaccio

300 g/11oz swordfish (one
    slice, cut into thin strips)
250 g/9 oz spinach
    (in leaves)
Rind of one pink grapefruit
5-6 radishes
Poppy seeds
1 lemon
Olive oil

Servings: 4
Preparation time: 15′
Difficulty: ●
Flavour: ●●
Kcal (per serving): 271
Proteins (per serving): 36
Fats (per serving): 12
Nutritional content: ●

Remove the rind from the pink grapefruit with a suitable utensil. Wash and dry the spinach, then chop it and arrange on the individual serving-dishes. Decorate each plate tastefully with the slices of swordfish, discs of radish and the pink grapefruit rind cut into thin strips. Sprinkle over a generous handful of poppy seeds and dress with olive oil, a little salt and lemon juice.

16 prawns
2 lemons
1 bunch chives
2 bunches rocket
2 tomatoes (to garnish)
Olive oil

Servings: 4	
Preparation time: 25' + 1h	
Difficulty: ●	
Flavour: ●●	
Kcal (per serving): 189	
Proteins (per serving): 15	
Fats (per serving): 11	
Nutritional content: ●	

CARPACCIO DI SCAMPI

Prawn carpaccio

Squeeze the lemons into a large bowl. Add the washed and finely-chopped chives, 4 tablespoons of top quality olive oil and a pinch of salt and work into a smooth paste with a wooden spoon. Clean the prawns and remove the heads (keeping a couple aside for decoration) and the shells, then tip the prawns into the marinade and leave for about an hour. Wash and dry the rocket and arrange it on a serving-dish. Place the prawns on top and spoon over the marinade. Garnish with slices of tomato.

INSALATA AL LARDO

Salad with bacon

1 Trim and wash the lettuce and chicory, drain well then chop into strips and tip into a bowl.

2 Dice the bacon fat and put it in a frying-pan with enough water to just cover the bottom of the pan and a clove of garlic, and sauté very gently.

3 As soon as the bacon fat begins to colour, add half a glass of vinegar and leave to boil for a couple of minutes. Tip the contents of the pan over the salad, season with salt and pepper and serve immediately. This flavoursome salad is a typical Friuli dish.

1 head of cappuchin
    (or iceberg) lettuce
2 heads of Treviso (long-
    leafed) red chicory
100 g/3¹/₂ oz bacon fat
    (in a single slice)
Vinegar
Garlic

Servings: 6	
Preparation time: 20′	
Cooking time: 10′	
Difficulty: ●	
Flavour: ●●●	
Kcal (per serving): 186	
Proteins (per serving): 3	
Fats (per serving): 17	
Nutritional content: ●●●	

RADICCHIO DI TREVISO IN INSALATA

Treviso red chicory salad

3 heads of Treviso (long-leafed) red chicory
4 bunches of young salad greens
3 heads of Belgian endive
2 carrots
4-5 wild boar sausages (preserved in oil)
2 Tomino (goats' milk) cheeses
100 g/3^1/$_2$ oz stoned black olives
Raw egg sauce
Olive oil

For the raw egg sauce
4 egg yolks
Powdered paprika (or chilli pepper)
Thyme
Olive oil

Servings: 4	
Preparation time: 15'	
Difficulty: ●	
Flavour: ●●	
Kcal (per serving): 1070	
Proteins (per serving): 46	
Fats (per serving): 93	
Nutritional content: ●●●	

Trim and wash the various salads, chop them up roughly and arrange on a serving-dish, lightly sprinkled with oil and salt. Distribute the sausages, cut as you prefer, the cheeses cut into disks, the grated carrots and the olives over the salad to make an attractive and colourful dish to set in the middle of the table and serve with the egg sauce in the centre.

To make the raw egg sauce, proceed c follows:

1 Whiz the egg yolks for a fair lengt of time in the food processor wit the thyme leaves, a drop of oil and pinch of salt.

2 Pour into a bowl, blend in a tabl spoon of paprika (or half of chil pepper) and 3 tablespoons of oil.

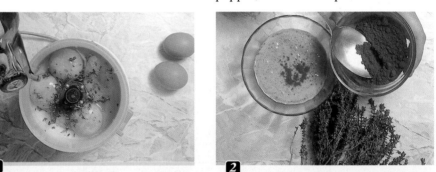

RADICCHIO DI CHIOGGIA CON I FAGIOLI

Chioggia red chicory with beans

2 heads (350-400 g/12-14 oz) of Chioggia (round) red chicory
250 g/9 oz borlotti or Lamon beans
150 g/5 oz bacon rind
Vinegar
Olive oil

Servings:	4-6
Preparation time:	15' + 5-6 h
Cooking time:	1h
Difficulty:	●
Flavour:	●●
Kcal (per serving):	428
Proteins (per serving):	17
Fats (per serving):	33
Nutritional content:	●●

1 Set the beans to steep at least 5-6 hours in advance; if you are using fresh beans, double the quantity. Set them in a casserole covered with lightly salted cold water, with the singed and scraped bacon rind. Cover the casserole and cook over a very slow heat for an hour. Meanwhile trim and wash the chicory.

2 When the beans are cooked the water should have been almost completely absorbed. Mash the beans into a pulp, remove the bacon rind and cut it into thin strips. Tip both into a large bowl with the chicory, season with salt, pepper, a hint of vinegar and a drop of oil.

RADICCHIO DI TREVISO FRITTO E GRIGLIATO

Treviso red chicory, fried and grilled

6 heads of Treviso (long-
    leafed) red chicory
2 eggs
Flour
Breadcrumbs
Olive oil
Oil for frying

Servings:	6
Preparation time:	15'
Cooking time:	1h
Difficulty:	●●
Flavour:	●●
Kcal (per serving):	500
Proteins (per serving):	10
Fats (per serving):	40
Nutritional content:	●●●

1 Trim and wash the heads of chicory, and remove the outer leaves from three of them – you can use these as a garnish or for salad – trim the tops and cut into quarters. Cut the remaining three heads in two lengthwise, without removing any of the leaves or trimming the tops.

2 Coat the quarter chicory heads lightly in flour, and then dip alternately in the beaten egg and bread-crumbs several times. Fry in plenty of boiling oil in a frying-pan.

3 Meanwhile dress the halved chicory heads with olive oil and season with salt, then cook on a very hot cast-iron grill pan.

VEGETABLES, SAVOURY FLANS AND EGGS

8

CAVOLO ALL'ACETO

Cabbage in vinegar

600 g/1¹/₄ lb white
   cabbage
2 stalks celery
1 clove garlic
100 g/3¹/₂ oz bacon fat
   (in one slice)
2 eggs
Flour
Breadcrumbs
Sugar
Vinegar
Oil for frying

Servings: 4	
Preparation time: 20′	
Cooking time: 50′	
Difficulty: ●●	
Flavour: ●●●	
Kcal (per serving): 669	
Proteins (per serving): 2	
Fats (per serving): 50	
Nutritional content: ●●●	

 **1** Trim the cabbage, removing the tough outer leaves, wash and blanch for fifteen minutes in lightly salted water. Drain and chop into strips about ¹/₂ cm/¹/₄ in wide. Trim the celery and chop into chunks.

2 Chop the bacon fat and sauté in a casserole with the garlic in about 4-5 tablespoons of oil; add the cabbage and stir well. Season with salt and pepper, then pour over half a glass of vinegar and half a glass of water.

3 Add half a teaspoon of sugar, stir in, then cover the casserole and simmer gently for 15 minutes to let the liquid reduce.

4 Drain the strips of cabbage, dip first in the beaten eggs and then in the breadcrumbs twice, then fry in plenty of boiling oil. Coat the chopped celery chunks in flour, then fry them too. Drain both on kitchen paper, sprinkle with salt and serve.

8 artichokes
1 lemon
Sugar
Olive oil

Servings: 6	
Preparation time: 20′	
Cooking time: 20′	
Difficulty: ●●	
Flavour: ●●	
Kcal (per serving): 326	
Proteins (per serving): 4	
Fats (per serving): 10	
Nutritional content: ●●	

CARCIOFI "IN TECIA"

Baked artichokes

Prepare the artichokes, removing the tougher outer leaves and trimming the stalk; plunge into cold water acidulated with a little lemon juice to prevent them going black. Drain them upside down, so that the water drips out of the spaces between the leaves, then set them upside down (with the stalk upwards) in a fireproof dish or pan with a glass of water, 5-6 tablespoons of oil and a pinch of salt. Cook over a lively heat for about 20 minutes (or alternatively in a pre-heated oven at 200 °C for half an hour). Half-way through cooking, add a little sugar. When cooked, leave to cool slightly before serving.

FAGIOLI IN SALSA

Beans in sauce

If you are using dried beans remember to set them to steep for 5-6 hours in advance. Drain and set in a casserole covered with cold, lightly salted water and simmer as slowly as possible for 50 minutes, then drain and tip into a bowl. Clean the anchovies, then wash and fillet them. Sauté the garlic cloves lightly in a frying-pan in 4-5 tablespoons of oil, remove them as soon as they begin to colour, and tip in the chopped anchovy fillets, breaking them up with a wooden spoon. Pour over 3-4 tablespoons of vinegar and mix, letting the flavours blend, then tip the resulting sauce over the beans and stir in well, adjusting salt and pepper to taste. Serve cold.

If you can't find the exquisite Lamon beans (named after the Belluno commune where they come from), you can use borlotti beans instead, which are similar though smaller and more floury.

500 g/1 lb 2 oz Lamon
    (or borlotti) beans
    (250 g/9 oz if dried)
6 anchovies
2 cloves garlic
Vinegar
Olive oil

Servings: 4	
Preparation time: 20' + 5-6 h	
Cooking time: about 1h	
Difficulty: ●●	
Flavour: ●●●	
Kcal (per serving): 552	
Proteins (per serving): 37	
Fats (per serving): 16	
Nutritional content: ●●	

Frittata all'aringa

Herring omelette

6 eggs
2 smoked herrings
Milk
Olive oil

Servings: 6	
Preparation time: 10' + 20'	
Cooking time: 20'	
Difficulty: ●●	
Flavour: ●●●	
Kcal (per serving): 504	
Proteins (per serving): 39	
Fats (per serving): 35	
Nutritional content: ●●	

Roast the herrings briefly on a very hot grill pan, then skin and trim them and chop into evenly-sized long strips. Beat the eggs in a bowl, and add a scant glass of milk, a hint of salt, pepper and the herring strips.

Leave the mixture to rest for 20 minutes, then heat 4-5 tablespoons of oil in a frying-pan without letting it smoke. Cook the omelette on one side for 6-7 minutes, then turn it over carefully using a plate and cook on the other side.

154

FRITTATA AI PISELLI

Pea omelette

Beat the eggs in a bowl along with a pinch of salt and pepper and a sprig of chopped parsley. Wash and dry the peas and add them to the egg mixture, then leave it to sit for a while. Melt the butter in a frying-pan with 3-4 tablespoons of oil, without letting it smoke, then pour in the omelette mixture. Cook on one side for 5-6 minutes, then turn over carefully with the help of a plate, cook on the other side and serve piping hot.

6 eggs
250 g/9 oz shelled peas
Parsley
30 g/1 oz butter
Olive oil

Servings: 6
Preparation time: 5' + 10'
Cooking time: 15'
Difficulty: ●●
Flavour: ●●
Kcal (per serving): 306
Proteins (per serving): 13
Fats (per serving): 24
Nutritional content: ●●

MELANZANE CON IL RISO

Stuffed aubergines

6 aubergines
80 g/3 oz rice
2 onions
20 g/²/3 oz pine kernels
20 g/²/3 oz raisins
Sugar
Powdered cinnamon
Vegetable stock (see p. 34)
Olive oil

Servings: 6-8	
Preparation time: 20'	
Cooking time: 50'	
Difficulty: ●●●	
Flavour: ●●●	
Kcal (per serving): 581	
Proteins (per serving): 16	
Fats (per serving): 36	
Nutritional content: ●●●	

1 Trim and peel the aubergines, cut them in two lengthwise and scoop out the centre with a spoon, keeping the flesh to one side. Blanch for 10 minutes in plenty of lightly salted water.

2 Peel the onions, chop them finely and sauté in a casserole in 4-5 tablespoons of oil. Add the chopped aubergine flesh, the rice and the pine kernels, and toast over a rapid heat for 3-4 minutes, then add a ladleful of hot vegetable stock.

3 Cook the rice by gradually pouring in ladlefuls of boiling stock: after 10 minutes add the raisins and a teaspoon of sugar. After another ten minutes the rice should be cooked. Fill the aubergine halves and arrange them in an ovenproof dish, sprinkle with cinnamon powder and grill in a pre-heated oven at 200 °C for 10 minutes.
This dish constitutes a meal in itself, rich in the Eastern flavours which pervade so much of Venetian cooking.

PATATE ALLA TRIESTINA

Trieste potato pancake

1 Boil and peel the potatoes. Peel the onion and slice it thinly, then sauté in a frying-pan in 2-3 tablespoons of oil, with the diced ham or bacon fat. Add the potatoes cut into slices.

2 Season with salt and pepper, then pour over a ladleful of stock. Lower the heat, and cook gently, letting the flavours blend, mashing the potatoes with a wooden spatula until you have a sort of pancake.

3 After 5-6 minutes, turn over carefully with the help of a plate, and cook the other side for the same time.

600 g/1¹/₄ lb potatoes
50 g/2 oz ham or bacon fat
1 onion
Vegetable stock (see p. 34)
Olive oil

Servings:	4
Preparation time:	15′
Cooking time:	40′
Difficulty:	●●
Flavour:	●●
Kcal (per serving):	353
Proteins (per serving):	4
Fats (per serving):	23
Nutritional content:	●●●

ZUCCA IN MARINATA

Marinated pumpkins

1 kg/2¹/4 lb yellow
    pumpkin
1 clove garlic
Basil
Vinegar
Olive oil

Servings: 6	
Preparation time: 15′ + 2-3h	
Cooking time: 35′	
Difficulty: ●	
Flavour: ●●	
Kcal (per serving): 107	
Proteins (per serving): 1	
Fats (per serving): 10	
Nutritional content: ●●	

1 Peel the pumpkin, halve it, remove seeds and filaments and cut into slices. Arrange these in a greased ovenproof dish, sprinkle lightly with salt and trickle with oil, then set the dish in a pre-heated oven at 160 °C for half an hour. Remove from the oven and arrange layers of pumpkin slices in a bowl, alternating them with layers of basil leaves.

2 Heat a glass of vinegar in a small saucepan with the garlic, salt and pepper. As soon as it comes to the boil pour it over the pumpkin and cover the bowl immediately. This delicious dish from Chioggia should be kept for at least 2-3 hours before serving.

1

2

FOCACCIA AL RADICCHIO

Red chicory pie

Pile the flour in the centre of a floured work surface, make a well in the centre and pour in the yeast dissolved in a little warm water along with a tablespoon of oil and a little salt. Knead together, adding enough warm water to produce a soft, springy dough. Wrap up in a clean, damp tea-cloth and leave to rise in a warm place for an hour.

Trim the chicory, then wash and dry it and chop up roughly. Sauté in a frying-pan in 4-5 tablespoons of oil with the garlic cloves and the chives. Pour over half a ladleful of stock, season with salt and pepper, then cover the pan and leave to cook for 10 minutes.

Take about four-fifths of the pastry dough and roll out a circle nearly double the size of the baking-tin or pie dish. Grease the dish with butter or oil, then line it with the pastry. Remove the cloves of garlic from the chicory and stir in a tablespoon of rinsed capers, the stoned olives and a pinch of chilli powder, then tip it into the pie dish. Roll out four broad strips with the remaining pastry and arrange crosswise on the top of the pie then fold the edges of the pastry inwards over the filling. Bake in a pre-heated oven at 200 °C for about 30 minutes and serve. The pie is also excellent cold.

600 g/1 1/4 lb red chicory (round or long-leafed)
50 g/2 oz salted capers
24 black olives
2 cloves garlic
Red chilli pepper (in powder)
Chives
Vegetable stock (see p. 34)
Olive oil

For the pastry
400 g/14 oz wholemeal flour
20 g/2/3 oz fresh yeast

Servings: 6
Preparation time: 30' + 1h
Cooking time: 40'
Difficulty: ●●●
Flavour: ●●
Kcal (per serving): 561
Proteins (per serving): 10
Fats (per serving): 26
Nutritional content: ●

TORTA DI ASPARAGI

Asparagus pie

1 Trim the asparagus, removing the woody part of the stem; steam for twenty minutes then chop. Melt the butter in a frying-pan, tip in the asparagus, season with salt and pepper and sauté for a couple of minutes then drain, tip into a bowl and leave to cool.

2 Using an egg-whisk or fork, in a bowl gently beat together the eggs, the bran, the cream and a pinch of salt and pepper.

The fertile hillside regions produce many of the foodstuffs used in local cooking.

250 g/9 oz shortcrust pastry (frozen will do)	Servings: 4	Fats (per serving): 60
	Preparation time: 20'	Nutritional content: ●●●
400 g/14 oz asparagus	Cooking time: 55'	
2 eggs	Difficulty: ●●●	
200 ml/6 fl oz/³/4 cup fresh cream	Flavour: ●●	
1 tablespoon bran	Kcal (per serving): 729	
30 g/1 oz butter	Proteins (per serving): 12	

3 Roll out the pastry to a thickness of about 5 mm/¹/4 in and cut into two rectangles, one larger than the other. Use the larger one to line a lightly greased baking-tin or pie dish, prick the pastry with a fork, then spread the asparagus over it.

4 Pour over this the egg and cream mixture, cover with the second rectangle of pastry, then fold over and seal the edges. Bake the pie in a pre-heated oven at 200 °C for a good half hour.

L "SMACAFÀM"

Sausage and bacon in batter

300 g/11 oz white flour
300 g/11 oz buckwheat
    flour
1 lucanica (or other fresh
    pork sausage, see p.
    101)
50 g/2 oz smoked bacon
50 g/2 oz bacon fat
Flour
1 litre/2 pints/4 cups milk
Salad or vegetables
    (to accompany)
30 g/1 oz butter
Olive oil

Servings: 6	
Preparation time: 15'	
Cooking time: 45'	
Difficulty: ●●	
Flavour: ●●●	
Kcal (per serving): 878	
Proteins (per serving): 23	
Fats (per serving): 44	
Nutritional content: ●●●	

1 In a bowl blend the flour with the milk, a tablespoon of oil and a pinch of salt. Sauté the diced bacon fat in a frying-pan in a trickle of water.

2 Mash up half the sausage meat and tip it into the flour and milk batter, then stir in half the diced bacon and the bacon fat with its juices and a pinch of pepper.

3 Pour the mixture into a greased and floured baking-tin or pie dish, scattering the top with slices of the remaining sausage and the diced bacon. Bake in a hot oven at 200 °C for about 40 minutes until it is nice and golden. Serve with salad or fresh vegetables.

This dish is traditionally eaten in Trentino around Carnival time, and is normally served with the wild salad known locally as dente di cane *(or* dog's tooth) *and elsewhere as* dente di leone *(or* lion's tooth). *This is none other than the common dandelion, also known as* insalata matta *(crazy salad).*

CAKES
AND BISCUITS

9

"BAÌCOLI" DI VENEZIA

Venetian toast biscuits

180 g/6 oz flour
10 g/^{1}/3 oz fresh yeast
Orange flower water
20 g/^{2}/3 oz sugar
Salt
20 g/^{2}/3 butter

Servings: 4	
Prep. time: 30' + 3h 30'	
Cooking time: 40'	
Difficulty: ●●●	
Kcal (per serving): 281	
Proteins (per serving): 4	
Fats (per serving): 5	
Nutritional content: ●●●	

1 Knead together 30g/1 oz of flour with the yeast diluted in 3 tablespoons of warm water. Work into a fairly stiff dough, roll into a ball, cut a cross on the top and leave to rest for half an hour wrapped in a tea-cloth.

2 Take the ball of dough, and knead in the remaining flour, with the butter cut into flakes, the sugar, a pinch of salt, a scant half-glass of water and a teaspoon of orange flower water. Knead well and divide into two halves.

3 Roll each section of dough into a slightly flattened sausage about 25 cm/10 in long. Lay on a baking tray and leave to rise for an hour covered with a clean tea-cloth, then bake in a pre-heated oven at 200 °C for about twenty minutes.

4 Leave to cool for a couple of hours, then cut diagonally into slices about 2 mm/^{1}/10 in thick and about 7 to 8 cm/3 in long. Lay the biscuits on a baking-tray and bake again in the oven at 200 °C for about 15 minutes until golden.

Like the following recipes, the method used here for the classic baìcoli biscuits involves the traditional kneading and rising procedures. Naturally these are more time-consuming, but well worth the trouble in view of the delicacy and flavour of the result.

"BIGARANI"

Ring biscuits

750 g/1 lb 10 oz flour
100 g/3¹/₂ oz sugar
2 eggs
30 g/1 oz fresh yeast
Milk
Salt
180 g/6 oz butter

Servings: 8	
Prep. time: 30' + 3h + 48h	
Cooking time: 25'	
Difficulty: ●●	
Kcal (per serving): 803	
Proteins (per serving): 14	
Fats (per serving): 27	
Nutritional content: ●●●	

1 Blend 50 g/2 oz of flour with the yeast diluted in a glass of warm milk. Roll the dough into a ball and leave to rest for an hour, then knead in the remaining flour, the sugar and a pinch of salt, along with 150 g/5 oz softened butter in flakes and the eggs. Knead well and roll into a ball, wrap up in a clean tea-cloth and leave to rise for 2 hours.

2 Divide the dough into pieces and roll into sausages of about 1 cm/¹/₂ in diameter and 18-20 cm/4 in long, then join the ends and shape into ovals.
Lay the bigarani on a greased baking-tray, flattening them a little, then bake in a pre-heated oven at 220 °C for about 15 minutes.
Remove them when they are golden then leave to rest for 48 hours, then re-bake in the oven at 200 °C for 10 minutes.
These biscuits keep well stored in hermetically-sealed glass containers.

L'"Bussolà" di Vicenza

Vicenza yeast cake

Pile the flour in the middle of a floured work-surface. Make a well in the centre and pour in the yeast diluted in a little warm water, the eggs, a pinch of salt and 80 g/3 oz of softened butter. Work the ingredients well together, and after a little while add a small glass of Marsala. Roll the dough into a ball, cover and leave to rise for an hour. Pile into a greased and floured ring-shaped cake tin. Melt the remaining butter, level off the surface of the cake and brush with the butter and sprinkle with sugar. Bake in a pre-heated oven at 190 °C for about an hour.

520 g/1 lb 2 oz flour
    (plus a little to sprinkle
    the cake tin)
6 eggs
20 g/²/3 oz fresh yeast
Sweet Marsala
Granulated sugar
Salt
120 g/4 oz butter

Servings:	6
Preparation time:	30' + 1h
Cooking time:	1h
Difficulty:	●●
Kcal (per serving):	937
Proteins (per serving):	18
Fats (per serving):	27
Nutritional content:	●●●

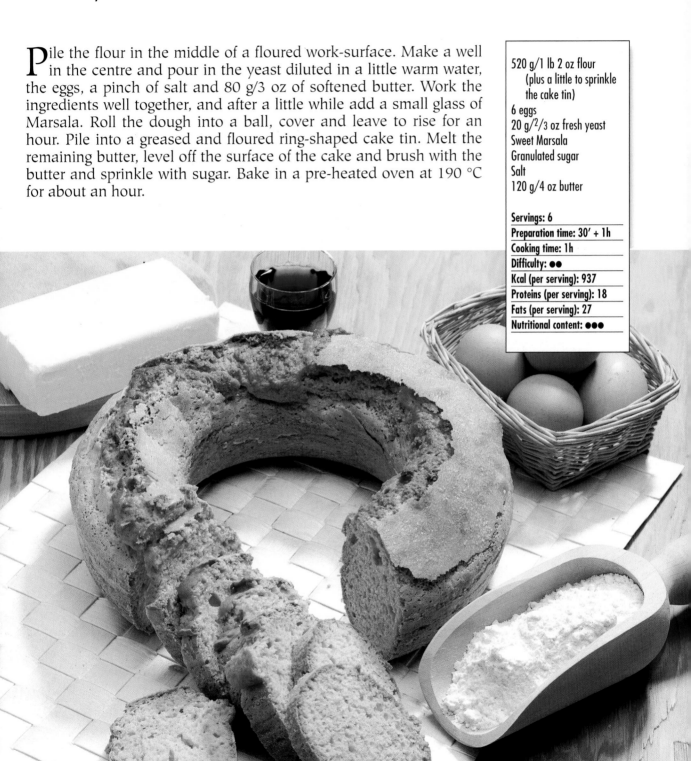

L"BUZOLÀI" DI CORMONS

Cormons egg pastries

560 g/1 lb 3 oz flour
5 eggs
70 g/2¹/₂ oz sugar
Salt
60 g/2 oz butter

Servings: 6	
Preparation time: 45' + 30'	
Cooking time: about 30'	
Difficulty: ●●	
Kcal (per serving): 721	
Proteins (per serving): 18	
Fats (per serving): 18	
Nutritional content: ●●●	

1 Melt 35 g/a generous ounce of butter in a bain-marie, then blend with the sugar and a pinch of salt. Pile the flour in the centre of a floured work surface, make a well in the centre and pour in the sugar and butter, break in the eggs and knead the dough energetically for 40 minutes.

2 Roll out into finger-size sausages about 30 cm/12 in long then leave to rest for about half an hour. After this flatten them slightly and form into rings. Arrange on two lightly greased baking-trays and bake in a pre-heated oven at 160 °C for 25 minutes, making sure that the pastries remain a delicate pale colour.

1

2

"CARAMÈI"

Caramelised fruit

Set the apricots and prunes to steep in warm water for 15 minutes before you start. Drain them, and chop into evenly-sized chunks.

In a small saucepan caramelise the sugar diluted with a glass of water. When it turns the right brown colour, lower the heat and tip in all the chopped fruit and nuts, along with the washed and dried grapes, and mix well so that all the pieces become nicely coated.

You can now use the caramelised fruits and nuts to make attractive and elegant arrangements spiked on wooden toothpicks, using the remaining caramel to bond the various ingredients together.

200 g/7 oz sugar
100 g/3¹/₂ oz grapes
120 g/4 oz dried apricots
100 g/3¹/₂ oz stoned
   prunes
100 g/3¹/₂ oz shelled
   almonds and hazelnuts
80 g/3 oz shelled walnuts

Servings:	4-6
Preparation time:	20' + 15'
Cooking time:	5'
Difficulty:	●
Kcal (per serving):	526
Proteins (per serving):	10
Fats (per serving):	21
Nutritional content:	●●●

CREMA FRITTA ALLA VENEZIANA

Venetian fried custard

100 g/3¹/₂ oz flour
2 eggs
200 g/7 oz sugar - plus
    extra sugar (optional)
    to decorate
1 litre/2 pints/4 cups milk
1 lemon
Breadcrumbs
Olive oil
Oil for frying

Servings: 4	
Preparation time: 20' + 24h	
Cooking time: 25'	
Difficulty: ●●	
Kcal (per serving): 921	
Proteins (per serving): 18	
Fats (per serving): 52	
Nutritional content: ●●●	

1 In a casserole, blend the egg yolks with the sugar, keeping the whites to one side. Delicately fold in the flour and the lemon juice, then gradually trickle in the milk. Set the casserole over a moderate heat.

2 When the batter comes to the boil, remove from the heat and turn out the contents onto a lightly-greased marble work-surface, spreading it out with a knife to a thickness of about 2 cm/1 in. The cream should then be left to rest at length, ideally for an entire day. After this, cut it into lozenges and dip into the egg whites and then the breadcrumbs, and fry in plenty of boiling oil. Serve immediately, dusting if you wish with extra sugar.

250 g/9 oz flour
1 egg
Sugar
20 g/²/3 oz fresh yeast
Milk (about ¹/2 litre/
    1 pint/2 cups)
1 lemon
Cinnamon
30 g/1 oz pine kernels
Salt
30 g/1 oz raisins
30 g/1 oz sultanas
50 g/2 oz vanilla-flavoured
    icing sugar
Rum
Oil for frying

Servings: 4	
Preparation time: 45' + 30'	
Cooking time: 20'	
Difficulty: ●●	
Kcal (per serving): 1142	
Proteins (per serving): 16	
Fats (per serving): 51	
Nutritional content: ●●●	

"FRÌTOLE"

Fruit fritters

1 Dilute the yeast in a little warm water, and mix with the eggs and two tablespoons of sugar. Incorporate the flour, the grated lemon rind, a pinch of cinnamon, a small glass of rum and enough milk to produce a fairly fluid batter.

2 Blend thoroughly with a wooden spatula for about half an hour, then add the raisins, the sultanas, and the pine kernels. Leave the mixture to rest for a further half hour, then drop spoonfuls into a frying-pan filled with plenty of boiling oil, making sure you rinse the spoon in hot water each time. Drain the golden fritters on kitchen paper, then dust generously with vanilla-flavoured icing-sugar.

1

2

FAGOTTINI DI VENEZIA

Venetian turnovers

1 Prepare the pastry: melt the butter in a small saucepan with two fingers of water, then leave to cool. Pile the flour on a work surface, make a well in the centre, pour in the butter and begin to blend it in, adding the icing sugar, the egg and the yolk, a pinch of salt and the grated lemon rind. Knead energetically for at least half an hour until you have a smooth, firm dough. Put in a bowl, cover with a cloth and set aside for an hour.

2 To make the filling, cream the butter then gradually beat in the sugar, the egg yolk and the flour.

3 Stir in the raisins, the diced candied peel and half a glass of rum, then gently fold in the stiffly-beaten egg white.

4 Roll the pastry out as thin as possible (it should not be more than 1/20 in thick), and use a pastry-wheel to cut out circles of a diameter of about 10 cm/4 in. Gather up the remaining pastry and roll out, and cut out more circles until it is all used up. Set a small spoonful of the filling in the centre of each, brush the edges with beaten egg yolk, then fold over not quite in half and seal the edges with one a little short of the other to form a sort of ridge. Press down each turnover lightly to flatten the base then line them up on a lightly greased baking tray and bake in a pre-heated oven at 180 °C for 35 minutes.

For the pastry	For the filling	Rum	Difficulty: ●●●
250 g/9 oz flour	75 g/3 oz flour	75 g/3 oz butter	Kcal (per serving): 771
1 egg and 1 yolk	75 g/3 oz sugar		Proteins (per serving): 19
1 lemon	1 egg and 1 yolk		Fats (per serving): 36
Salt	20 g/^{2}/3 oz sultanas	Servings: 4	Nutritional content: ●●●
35 g/1 oz icing sugar	30 g/1 oz candied orange	Preparation time: 50' + 1h	
50 g/2 oz butter	peel	Cooking time: 35'	

"FREGOLATA"

Almond balls

250 g/9 oz flour (plus a little to sprinkle the oven dish)
2 eggs
250 g/9 oz sugar
250 g/9 oz shelled almonds
Milk
Salt
50 g/2 oz butter

Servings:	4-6
Preparation time:	50' + 15'
Cooking time:	30'
Difficulty:	●●
Kcal (per serving):	811
Proteins (per serving):	24
Fats (per serving):	34
Nutritional content:	●●●

1 Toast the almonds in the oven, remove the skin and grind them in the food processor.

2 On a floured work-surface mix the flour with the sugar, the ground almonds and a pinch of salt, then add 25 g/1 oz melted butter and the beaten eggs.

3 Knead well, adding a scant glass of milk and working until you have a firm, pliable dough, then set aside for a quarter of an hour.

4 Roll into balls about the size of a walnut and line up in a buttered and floured ovenproof dish. Bake the fregolata in a pre-heated oven at 200 °C for 25 minutes until nicely browned.

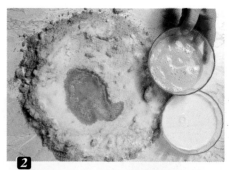

Venetian masks and sweetmeats, two typical aspects of the lagoon city illustrated in an eighteenth-century painting by Pietro Longhi.

L "GALANI"

Fried pastries

500 g/1 lb 2 oz flour
30 g/1 oz butter
1 egg and 2 yolks
Sugar (granulated and
    icing)
Salt
Dry white wine
Oil for frying

Servings:	4-6
Preparation time:	30′ + 15′
Cooking time:	20′
Difficulty:	●●
Kcal (per serving):	729
Proteins (per serving):	15
Fats (per serving):	45
Nutritional content:	●●●

1 Pile the flour in the centre of a floured work surface, make a well in the centre and break in the egg and yolks, along with the butter at room temperature and cut into flakes, a tablespoon of sugar and a pinch of salt. Knead energetically and at length, adding a glass of wine, until you have a firm, pliable dough.

2 Leave the pastry to rest for about a quarter of an hour, then roll it out very thin. Use a pastry-wheel to cut it into strips of whatever length you wish, forming them into varied shapes. Fry in a frying-pan in plenty of boiling oil, removing as soon as they are a pale, golden colour. Set the galani on a serving-plate and sprinkle generously with icing sugar. In Venice these sweetmeats are traditionally eaten cold on Maundy Thursday.

1

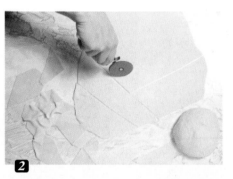

2

GNOCCHI DI ALBICOCCHE

Apricot gnocchi

16 apricots
1 kg/2^1/$_4$ lb potatoes
250 g/9 oz flour
3 eggs
100 g/3^1/$_2$ oz
   breadcrumbs
Sugar
200 g/7 oz butter

Servings: 4-6	
Preparation time: 30' + 10'	
Cooking time: 45'	
Difficulty: ●●●	
Kcal (per serving): 1072	
Proteins (per serving): 23	
Fats (per serving): 51	
Nutritional content: ●●●	

Wash the apricots, open them to remove the stone then close them up again. Boil and peel the potatoes, mash and leave to cool, then blend with the flour, the eggs, a knob of butter and a pinch of salt. Leave the dough to rest for about ten minutes, then break off pieces and use to cover each of the apricots. Drop the gnocchi one by one into a large pot of very lightly salted water, removing them with a slatted spoon as soon as they come to the surface. Melt the remaining butter in a small saucepan then stir in the breadcrumbs. Drop the gnocchi into the saucepan one by one as you drain them, rolling them round until they are covered in breadcrumbs, then serve sprinkled with sugar.

"GUBANA" DI CIVIDALE

Cividale fruit ring

1 Set the raisins and sultanas to steep in the rum. Prepare the pastry by rubbing the butter into the flour and adding a scant glass of water, a pinch of salt and 2 tablespoons of grappa or gin. Knead energetically for 10 minutes, then roll the pastry into a ball and leave to rest for 15 minutes. Repeat the kneading and resting 3 times, leaving the pastry to rest for half an hour after the last kneading.

For the pastry	250 g/9 oz sultanas	50 g/2 oz plain chocolate	Preparation time: 50' + 1h
250 g/9 oz flour	100 g/3½ oz pine	50 g/2 oz candied lime	Cooking time: 30'
250 g/9 oz butter	kernels	2-3 dry biscuits	Difficulty: ●●●
Salt	6-8 dried figs	Grappa (or gin), rum	Kcal (per serving): 1335
250 g/9 oz shelled	6-8 dried prunes	Olive Oil	Proteins (per serving): 34
walnuts	1 lemon (or 1 orange)		Fats (per serving): 64
250 g/9 oz raisins	1 egg	Servings: 6	Nutritional content: ●●●

2 Meanwhile start on the filling. Chop finely in the food processor the walnuts, the pine kernels, the candied lime, the chocolate, the raisins and sultanas, the figs and the stoned prunes. Tip into a bowl and mix in the grated lemon (or orange) rind and the finely crumbled biscuits, then fold in the stiffly-beaten egg white.

3 Roll out the pastry as thinly as possible, then spread the filling evenly over it, leaving the edges free. Roll it up like a Swiss-roll, then join the ends to form a ring. Set on a greased baking-tray, brush with the beaten egg yolk and bake in a pre-heated oven at 200 °C for half an hour.

PANDORO DI VERONA

1 In a bowl, dilute the yeast in a tablespoon of warm water, then blend in a heaped table-spoon of flour. Leave to rise for about 20 minutes.

2 In another bowl, mix 65 g/2¹/₂ oz flour with a tablespoon of sugar, incorporate 1 egg and 1 yolk, 10 g/¹/₃ oz of melted butter and the leavening base (see step 1). Mix well for 4-5 minutes then cover the bowl with a clean tea-cloth and leave to rise for an hour.

3 Take a larger bowl and blend together 130 g/4¹/₂ oz flour, another two tablespoons of sugar, 20 g/²/₃ oz of melted butter, one egg, 2 yolks, a drop of vanilla essence and a pinch of salt. In-corporate the leavening base (see step 2), tip onto a floured work surface and knead energetically for 10 minutes till you have a light, pliable dough.

4 Gradually work another 50 g/2 oz flour into the dough, until it becomes soft and loses all sticki-ness. Form into a ball, cover, and leave to rise for at least 3 hours. .

5 Roll the dough out into a rec-tangle and distribute over it 150 g/5 oz butter in flakes. Fold the edges in over the butter, then roll out the dough not too fine. Fold it in three, then roll out again. Repeat this operation, then leave to rest for 20 minutes. Roll and fold the dough twice again, then leave to rest for a further 20 minutes.

275 g/10 oz flour (plus flour for rolling out) 80 g/3 oz sugar (plus sugar for dusting the cake tin) 2 eggs and 3 yolks 10 g/¹/₃ oz fresh yeast	Vanilla essence 180 g/6 oz butter (plus butter for greasing the cake tin) Salt Icing sugar	Servings: 4	Nutritional content: ●●●
		Prep. time: 1h + 5h 20'	
		Cooking time: 40'	
		Difficulty: ●●●	
		Kcal (per serving): 947	
		Proteins (per serving): 21	
		Fats (per serving): 55	

6 Set the dough on a well-floured work surface and begin to knead again delicately, using the palms of your hands and gentle rotating movements. Set it in a special pandoro cake tin, duly buttered and sprinkled with sugar, and bake in a pre-heated oven at 180 °C for about half an hour. Remove from the oven, leave to cool, then sprinkle generously with icing-sugar.

"POTIZZA"

Honey and walnut cake

1 Dilute the yeast in half a glass of warm milk and blend with 3 tablespoons of flour and a teaspoon of sugar. Leave to rise for 20 minutes. Meanwhile set the raisins to steep in warm water.

2 In a bowl beat 100 g/3½ oz butter to a cream, then delicately incorporate the eggs one by one. After the last egg, add 100 g/3½ oz sugar, the remaining flour and the leavening base (see step 1). Tip onto a floured work surface and knead until you have a pliable, not too stiff dough. Roll out as thinly as possible (on top of a floured tea-cloth if you like, since this will help with the subsequent rolling up).

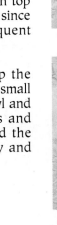

3 In the food processor chop the walnuts sprinkled with half a small glass of rum, then tip into a bowl and mix with the squeezed raisins and 100 g/3½ oz of sugar. Spread the mixture evenly over the pastry and cover with honey.

500 g/1 lb 2 oz flour (plus flour for rolling out and flouring the pie dish)	Milk	sugar	Kcal (per serving): 983
3 eggs	250 g/9 oz shelled walnuts	120 g/4 oz butter	Proteins (per serving): 16
30 g/1 oz fresh yeast	100 g raisins		Fats (per serving): 27
200 g/7 oz honey	Rum	Servings: 6	Nutritional content: ●●●
	Sugar	Preparation time: 1h + 1h	
	Vanilla-flavoured icing	Cooking time: 45'	
		Difficulty: ●●●	

4 Roll up like a Swiss-roll, join the ends to form a ring and set in a buttered and floured pie dish. Leave to rise until the dough reaches the top of the dish, then bake in a pre-heated oven at 180 °C for three-quarters of an hour. Remove, and sprinkle with vanilla-flavoured icing-sugar.

PAN DOLCE DI RISO TIROLESE

Tyrolese rice cake

200 g/7 oz rice
1 litre/2 pints/ 4 cups milk
250 g/9 oz sugar
8 eggs
150 g/5 oz sultanas
150 g/5 oz candied lime
Icing sugar to decorate
A pinch of salt
230 g/8 oz butter

Servings: 6-8	
Preparation time: 20'	
Cooking time: 1h	
Difficulty: ●●	
Kcal (per serving): 1016	
Proteins (per serving): 19	
Fats (per serving): 47	
Nutritional content: ●●●	

Set the rice in a casserole with the milk, the chopped lemon rind and the salt. Cover and cook over a very gentle heat for about 40 minutes, without stirring.

When the rice is cooked, tip it into a large bowl and incorporate the sugar and 200 g/7 oz of butter. Stir in the 8 egg yolks, then fold in the stiffly-beaten whites. Stirring delicately, add the washed and squeezed sultanas and the chopped candied lime.

Butter a cake tin, pour in the mixture and bake in a pre-heated oven at 160-180 °C for 30 minutes. When cooked, remove from the oven, and dust with icing sugar. The rice cake can be served either hot or cold, and is perfect for breakfast or for tea.

"STRUCCOLI" ALLA CARSOLINA

Carso mince pudding

1 Set the raisins to steep in warm water before starting. Knead the flour with the egg and enough water to produce a smooth, stiff dough. Roll it out not too thin, then pour over 60 g/2 oz of melted butter and sprinkle with the breadcrumbs, the sugar, the pine kernels, the squeezed raisins and the grated carobs.

2 Roll up like a Swiss roll then wrap the roll in a clean tea-cloth and tie the two ends with string. Bring a large saucepan of lightly salted water to the boil, immerse the "sausage" and simmer for 40 minutes. Remove the tea-cloth, cut into slices and arrange on a serving-dish. Prepare a sauce using 90 g/3 oz of melted butter blended with the vanilla-flavoured sugar and a pinch of cinnamon. Pour over and serve immediately.

250 g/9 oz flour
100 g/3^{1}/$_{2}$ oz sugar
1 egg
100 g/3^{1}/$_{2}$ oz breadcrumbs
80 g/3 oz raisins
80 g/3 oz pine kernels
4 dry carobs
Cinnamon
60 g/2 oz vanilla-flavoured icing sugar
150 g/5 oz butter

Servings: 4-6	
Preparation time: 30' + 15'	
Cooking time: 40'	
Difficulty: ●●	
Kcal (per serving): 888	
Proteins (per serving): 19	
Fats (per serving): 41	
Nutritional content: ●●●	

TESTA DI MORO (MOHRENKOPFE)

Chocolate chestnut pudding

400 g/14 oz dried
   chestnuts
1 litre/2 pints/4 cups milk
100 g/3 1/2 oz bitter (dark)
   chocolate
100 g/3 1/2 oz sugar
Rum
Whipped cream and liqueur
   cherries (to decorate)

Servings: 4-6	
Prep. time: 20' + 8h + 3-4h	
Cooking time: 40'	
Difficulty: ●●	
Kcal (per serving): 1185	
Proteins (per serving): 11	
Fats (per serving): 49	
Nutritional content: ●●●	

1 Set the chestnuts to steep in the milk 8 hours before you start. After this, cook them slowly in a covered pot in the milk, which they will almost completely absorb.

2 Drain the chestnuts, remove the outer skin and whiz in the food processor. Tip the purée into a bowl, and stir in the grated chocolate, the sugar and a glass of rum. Spoon the mixture into individual glass bowls, decorating with whipped cream and topping each with a cherry.
Set in the fridge for 3-4 hours before serving chilled, but not frozen.

TIRAMISÙ

(Coffee trifle)

Separate the egg yolks from the whites, put the yolks in a bowl with the sugar and beat with an electric whisk.
Add the mascarpone or cream cheese, and blend in slowly and very gently, then delicately fold in the stiffly-beaten whites.
Soak the sponge fingers in the coffee and arrange them in the bottom of a trifle-dish (or in individual dishes), then cover with the mascarpone cream. Put in the fridge for a couple of hours (in a section which is not too cold), before serving decorated with coffee beans.

500 g/1 lb 2 oz mascarpone (or cream cheese)
6 eggs
150 g/5 oz sugar
36 sponge fingers
Strong coffee
Servings: 8-10
Preparation time: 20' + 2h
Difficulty: ●●
Kcal (per serving): 916
Proteins (per serving): 24
Fats (per serving): 48
Nutritional content: ●●●

TORTA TRIESTINA

Trieste cake

5 eggs and 2 yolks
250 g/9 oz sugar
150 g/5 oz shelled almonds
200 g/7 oz dark chocolate
Flour
180 g/6 oz butter

Servings: 4-6	
Preparation time: 30′	
Cooking time: 50′	
Difficulty: ●●	
Kcal (per serving): 1269	
Proteins (per serving): 26	
Fats (per serving): 95	
Nutritional content: ●●●	

*The city and port
of Trieste in an old print.*

1 Beat the egg yolks with the sugar until thick and creamy, then fold in half the grated chocolate, 100 g/3 1/2 oz of the almonds, ground, and the stiffly-beaten egg whites. Spoon the mixture into a well-buttered and floured cake tin and bake in a pre-heated oven at 160 °C for three-quarters of an hour. Skin the remaining almonds and toast them in the oven for 10 minutes.

2 Remove the cake from the oven and ease it out of the tin. Leave to cool then cut into three layers of the same height. Chop the toasted almonds in the food processor.

3 Cream the remaining butter and sugar in a bowl, then stir in the other half of the grated chocolate and the two egg yolks.

4 Mix the cream delicately, then spread it on the two intermediate layers and put the cake back together. Spread the top and sides of the cake with the cream, then sprinkle with the chopped toasted almonds.

L "ZALETI"

Fruit biscuits

350 g/12 oz cornmeal
90 g/3 oz white flour
180 g/6 oz sugar
3 eggs and 1 yolk
100 g/3^1/$_2$ oz raisins
50 g/2 oz pine kernels
Rum
1 lemon
Milk
Baking soda
140 g/5 oz butter

Servings: 4-6	
Preparation time: 30' + 30'	
Cooking time: 30'	
Difficulty: ●●	
Kcal (per serving): 1310	
Proteins (per serving): 25	
Fats (per serving): 45	
Nutritional content: ●●●	

Set the raisins to steep in warm water half an hour before starting. Mix the two types of flour with two eggs and 1 yolk, the sugar and 120 g/4 oz of butter, adding a glass of warm milk in which you have dissolved a pinch of baking powder. Mix thoroughly, then add the squeezed raisins, the pine kernels, the grated lemon rind, and sprinkle in a small glass of rum.

Spoon the mixture into a piping bag and squeeze out the biscuits in different shapes (horseshoes, crescents, letters of the alphabet, numbers and so on) onto a lightly-buttered baking-tray. Otherwise you can roll out the mixture and cut it into strips or squares. After this, brush them with beaten egg, sprinkle with sugar and bake in a pre-heated oven at 160 °C for half an hour.

220 g/8 oz wholemeal flour	
10 g/¹/3 oz fresh yeast	
80 g/3 oz dried figs	
50 g/2 oz shelled walnuts	
50 g/2 oz shelled hazelnuts	
1 orange	
80 g/3 oz sultanas	
2 eggs	
Brandy	
150 g/5 oz sugar	
Milk	
100 g/3¹/2 oz butter	

Servings: 4	
Preparation time: 30' + 30'	
Cooking time: 45'	
Difficulty: ●●	
Kcal (per serving): 1066	
Proteins (per serving): 18	
Fats (per serving): 41	
Nutritional content: ●●●	

L "ZELTEN"

Wholemeal fruit cake

In a bowl beat the egg yolks and the sugar until thick and creamy. Fold in 80 g/3 oz of butter cut into flakes, a glass of milk, the yeast and finally, a little at a time and stirring gently all the time, 200 g/7 oz of flour. Add the juice of the orange and the grated rind, stir in well and then add a small glass of brandy. Gradually stir in the sultanas, the walnuts, the hazelnuts and the chopped figs. Leave the mixture to rest for half an hour.

Fold in the stiffly-beaten egg whites, then spoon into a buttered and floured cake tin. Bake in a pre-heated oven at 180 °C for 45 minutes, then serve. This cake is delicious served as a snack, or for tea with cream or jam.